Kingston

The IBM Years

The Friends of Historic Kingston

Kingston

The IBM Years

The Friends of Historic Kingston

Contributors

Ward L.E. Mintz, *project editor*

Harvey K. Flad

Roger Panetta, *guest scholar and editor*

Lowell Thing

Hugh Reynolds

Gail Godwin and Frances Halsband

William B. Rhoads

George G. Washington

BLACK · DOME

Published by Black Dome Press Corp.
649 Delaware Ave., Delmar, N.Y. 12054
blackdomepress.com, (518) 439-6512

First Edition Paperback 2014

ISBN: 978-1-883789-76-3

Library of Congress Control Number: 2014936987

Kingston—The IBM Years was made possible with support from the Architecture, Planning and Design Program
of the New York State Council on the Arts, with the support of Governor Andrew Cuomo and the New York State
Legislature; the County of Ulster's Ulster County Cultural Services & Promotion Fund administered by Arts
Mid-Hudson; the New York Council for the Humanities; the Mid-Hudson Valley Federal Credit Union; and three
anonymous donors.

New York Council for the Humanities

This book was made possible in part through a grant from
Furthermore: a program of the J.M. Kaplan Fund.

Front cover photograph: IBM Kingston Plant. Collection of the Friends of Historic Kingston.

Back cover photographs: Top (left to right): SAGE Test Cell Area, IBM Kingston. Courtesy of IBM; "Survival
under Nuclear Attack." The Official U.S. Government Booklet; Ulster County Office Building. Photograph
2013 by Stephen Benson. Background: Aerial photograph of IBM Kingston plant 1966. Collection of
Friends of Historic Kingston.

Design: Toelke Associates, www.toelkeassociates.com

Printed in the USA

10 9 8 7 6 5 4 3 2 1

Contents

The Friends of Historic Kingston

Kingston, New York, has a long and eventful history that includes the building of the Stockade by the Dutch in 1658, the burning of the city by the British in the Revolutionary War, and the building of the D&H Canal, which led to the development of the Rondout waterfront. Many architectural treasures remain—the old stone houses, the Courthouse, Old Dutch Church, Kingston City Hall, the Kingston High School, Carnegie Library, the stately homes on West Chestnut Street, the Rondout churches, and the row of the West Strand commercial buildings.

The Friends of Historic Kingston was organized in 1965 and is dedicated to the preservation of sites of historical and architectural significance within the City of Kingston, the education of the public about the heritage and beauty of the city, and the acquisition and conservation of materials relating to local history

To fulfill its mission the Friends has purchased, renovated and resold threatened historic properties. It successfully advocated for the renovation of the Kingston City Hall. It has taken the lead in obtaining New York State and National Historic Register designations for four historic districts and numerous buildings in our city. Frog Alley Park with its Louw-Bogardus House ruin is owned by the Friends of Historic Kingston. The house is currently undergoing an architectural and engineering assessment to determine how it might best be preserved and utilized as an educational site.

The Friends of Historic Kingston oversees two museums at the corner of Main and Wall Streets. The Federal-style Fred J. Johnston House (c. 1812) features eighteenth- and early-nineteenth-century furnishings in eight elegant room settings. The adjacent Museum features a gallery where annual exhibits relating to Kingston history are produced.

Other activities include walking tours of the Stockade area and the Rondout, Johnston House tours, lecture series, sponsorship of special events, and the publication of books on Kingston's history and architecture. Each year Preservation Awards are given to citizens and organizations who have preserved and restored their buildings.

Our newly redeveloped Web site (www.FOHK.org) provides an attractive and comprehensive look for those interested in exploring Kingston's historic areas and learning of our events. Our Facebook page features both current and archival photographs of Kingston.

We are pleased to present this year's Friends of Historic Kingston exhibit, "Kingston—The IBM Years," and we are excited about the publication of this insightful book that covers a significant period in Kingston's recent history. Special thanks are due Friends of Historic Kingston Board Member Ward Mintz, who conceived this project and devoted a tremendous amount of thought, time and energy to making this become a reality, and thereby, along with many other Board members and volunteers, and former IBM employees brought "Kingston—The IBM Years" to fruition.

Jane Kellar
Executive Director

J. Peter Roberts
President

Among IBMers who campaigned in 1975 with the Friends of Historic Kingston to save Kingston's historic City Hall were Jerry Leatherman, Paul Scogna, Lowell Thing, and John Weber.

Top: Boice Farm, Town of Ulster, n.d., site of the future IBM Plant. Collection of John F. Matthews. Bottom: Looking north up Broadway, Rondout, 1960s. As a result of Urban Renewal, the east (right) side of Broadway was demolished.

Top: Aerial view of IBM Kingston plant with Kingston-Rhinecliff Bridge in background, n.d.. Collection of John F. Matthews. Bottom: Kingston IBM Plant, walkway between Main Building (right) and Building 201 Lab. Photograph 2013 by Stephen Benson.

Raising the letter "I" for the IBM sign above the front entrance of IBM Kingston. Collection of John F. Matthews.

Preface and Acknowledgments

It was personal curiosity that first inspired this project to document the era of IBM's presence in Kingston. As a relative newcomer to Ulster County (in Kingston terms—only twenty-five years), I did not experience firsthand the opening of the IBM plant in the Town of Ulster and the arrival of thousands of workers and their families. I counted no employees of IBM Kingston among my friends. But I have a strong recollection of the announcement in 1994 of the closing of the IBM plant and my thoughts about the impact the closing would have on its workers and the county's economy. I would drive by the former IBM plant frequently, wondering what life was like during IBM's heyday. People told me that laid-off IBMers lived in neighborhoods like Rolling Meadows in the Town of Hurley and Hillside Acres in the Town of Ulster, and I wondered how they were faring. Those residential areas and the many others that were created when IBM moved to Kingston are reflective of another interest—architectural history. It was gratifying to be asked to join the Board of the Friends of Historic Kingston where I could indulge that passion. It all came together—an opportunity to create a project that examined IBM Kingston, the accomplishments of its workers, the lives they lived and where they lived them. The Friends Board thought it was a good idea and *Kingston—The IBM Years* was born.

It may be surprising to some that an exhibition has been organized that documents the history of an era—the IBM era—that ended only twenty years ago. In Kingston, "history" usually means the establishment of the Dutch settlement of Wiltwyck in the mid-1600s, or Kingston's designation as New York State's first capital and its subsequent burning by the British in 1777.

View of Island Dock with coal piles from the Delaware & Hudson Canal in the Rondout Creek. Collection Friends of Historic Kingston.

1

Presenting an exhibition about the early 1800s might also be expected, as Kingston's prominence as a Hudson River port was established in 1828 when the Delaware and Hudson Canal (D&H) opened for the shipment of coal from mines in Pennsylvania to the terminus in Kingston.

Why do an exhibition about the years from 1955 to 1994, when IBM operated its plant just outside the city in the Town of Ulster? For lovers of traditional history, no "great men" were involved and no wars were fought. But there were extraordinary technical and engineering achievements made possible by talented men and women and inspired leadership. Indeed, Kingston's IBM years are likely to have been the most important period in the city's industrial history since the D&H Canal's opening.

But it is more than that. Usually, when we study and present history, we rely mostly on written records and the memories of a few elderly people. For *Kingston—The IBM Years*, we are able to document a forty-year era that ended almost twenty years ago because there are still hundreds, even thousands, of people who remember it, whose lives were affected and who carry around vivid memories of that time. A significant number of them have been willing to share those memories through oral histories and search their mementoes for items that could help tell the story. It is their generosity that makes it possible for us to present this material to a broader audience.

Kingston Daily Freeman, December 31, 1955. Courtesy Daily Freeman.

IBM's plant and the thousands of employees who worked in it changed the physical landscape of Kingston and Ulster County. People came from all over the United States to work here, and people already living in the region were able to find employment. Entire neighborhoods sprang up, with schools and other community facilities to serve them. New professionals and businesses opened offices and stores in Kingston and the surrounding region. Houses of worship were built, as well as commercial buildings, especially strip developments and shopping centers.

Ulster County built itself a new office building, and the City of Kingston built a new City Hall. IBM employees, encouraged by supporting company policies, made themselves available as volunteers to local nonprofits. Their employer provided not-for-profit organizations with needed financial support.

It is one thing to learn the statistics about, say, the doubling of the Town of Ulster's population in one decade or the fact that 7,100 people worked in a 2.5-million-square-foot facility. It's another thing to delve deeper and discover what a career spent working for IBM was like, and what professional opportunities were available when one worked for one of the most successful and paternalistic companies in American history. It has also been possible to discover the experiences of people who didn't work for IBM but who read the scores of articles about IBM in the *Daily Freeman*, and who interacted with IBM and IBMers in stores, businesses, schools and professional offices.

Kingston—The IBM Years is not the last word on Kingston's history and growth in the twentieth century. Instead, it begins the conversation, allowing visitors from throughout the region to see the images and read the documentation, some refreshing their memories about what their lives were like and others looking with new eyes at their neighborhoods and the places at which they shop or worship. It is a chance for younger people

Britts, Kingston Plaza, late 1960s.

Employe Pledge
John Porsch, Kingston IBM Club vice president, (L9, presents an employe pledge of $95,500 to Elsie Richter, chairwoman of the industrial division of Ulster County United Way. Looking on are David Dittman, United Way 1976 campaign fund chairman (standing) and Dick Woodward, IBM Club president. (Freeman photo)

Kingston Daily Freeman, *November 13, 1975.*
Courtesy Daily Freeman.

to get a better idea of what their elders' lives were like. And we hope that our exhibition will attract other scholars to use the materials we have discovered, assembled and preserved for future studies of the era.

On one hand, *Kingston—The IBM Years* attempts to take the visitor and reader inside the IBM plant to get an idea of the impressive projects workers there were involved with—projects like SAGE (Semi-Automatic Ground Environment), the nation's air defense system that was developed in Kingston; the SABRE airline reservation system; and the 7090 data processing system that gave special attention to the needs of engineers and scientists. The Kingston plant was intimately involved with IBM's celebrated System 360 computers, which Kingston workers assembled, tested, shipped and supported, and also with the 3270 terminal, which was used to communicate with IBM mainframes. The exhibition attempts to give a sense of the complexity of the operation in Kingston, the range of job responsibilities, and the degree of training and travel available to some workers.

On the other hand, the exhibition looks outside the plant to see where workers relaxed and partied and where and how they lived. It remembers the Family Days on the grounds of the plant and the subsequent development of the IBM Recreation Center on Kukuk Lane in the Town of Ulster.

It acknowledges the hours of volunteer work IBMers gave to community institutions and local governments. IBMers lived all over the region: across the Hudson in communities like Red Hook, which was linked more closely to the IBM plant when the Kingston-Rhinecliff Bridge was completed

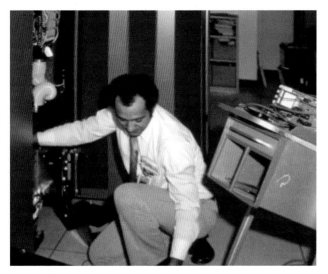

IBM recruited Steve Sorell in Providence, R.I., and he moved to Kingston with his family. Here he is working on an IBM 3420 Tape Drive, 1978. Photo by Bruce Whistance.

Steve Sorrell enjoying his electronics hobby on a work bench at home, 1978. Photo by Bruce Whistance.

in 1957; in old and new dwellings in the City of Kingston; and in new housing developments like Rolling Meadows in the Town of Hurley, and Whittier, Halcyon Park and Hillside Acres in the Town of Ulster. Indeed, as the recent Town of Ulster Comprehensive Plan notes, "… 78% of the Town of Ulster's housing stock was constructed after the arrival of IBM."

The built environment is important to the Friends of Historic Kingston, with its mission to support and protect the city's architectural, historical and cultural heritage, as it is to other Ulster County history and preservation organizations and commissions. Our organizations and commissions tend to prefer concentrating our energies on the preservation

IBM Kingston Family Day. View from a car of the "Octopus ride" with residential homes on Boice's Lane in background, 1958. Collection of Bruce Whistance.

IBM Recreational Center Pool on Kukuk Lane (screenshot), from "County of Contrasts," IBM promotional film, circa 1969.

Advertisement for homes in Whittier, Town of Ulster, screenshot from page of Daily Freeman, June 1957.

and interpretation of older neighborhoods with stone houses or neighborhoods that reflect earlier industries that connect us to the Hudson River and D&H Canal. We have rarely focused on the broader historical developments of the late nineteenth and twentieth centuries—the railroad and automobile eras—and how they changed our community. But we have an opportunity and responsibility to reflect the shifts in priorities in the fields of history and historic preservation that now encourage an interest in documenting and preserving later architecture, both commercial and residential. Currently, the Preservation League of New York State, in its Seven to Save program, implores communities to pay greater attention to "threats to historic resources built after World War II, such as buildings, neighborhoods, landscapes, and public and private sector complexes." We hope that Kingston—The IBM Years will help inspire and inform future action and programming.

Kingston—The IBM Years is the most complicated and expensive programming initiative that the Friends of Historic Kingston has undertaken. We are grateful to our funders—government, corporate and individual—for their support. We must thank especially the staff and panel of the Architecture, Planning and Design Program of the New York State Council on the Arts, which has supported both the planning and implementation phases of the project. We are also grateful for the grant from the Ulster County Cultural Services and Promotion Fund, supported by the County Legislature and administered by Arts Mid-Hudson, previously known as the Dutchess County Arts Council. The New York Council for the Humanities has also provided critical planning dollars. Three anonymous donors have lent their support. And not least, we want to thank our corporate funder, the Mid-Hudson Valley Federal Credit Union, which began its life in 1963 as the IBM Kingston Employees Federal Credit Union. There could be no more perfect partnership.

Just as important, this project could not have been completed without the involvement of many people. First, we thank Jane Kellar, the Friends of Historic Kingston's Executive Director, whose organizational talents, leadership abilities and good sense made this project possible. Roger Panetta, our esteemed guest scholar, introduced us to a methodology—the oral history interview—from which he has crafted a fascinating history. Stephen Benson's photographs made telling the story of Kingston's mid-century architecture a pleasure.

Ken Gray has produced a handsome exhibition, and Carol Garfinkel and Frank Futral gave important professional assistance. Peter Roberts supported our efforts not only as President of the Friends Board, but also through oral histories, coordination with catalogue essayists, involvement with the printing of images and his experience as a lifelong Kingston resident. Our Advisory Committee offered important direction, and we thank architect Frances Halsband, geographer Harvey Flad, historian Edwin Ford and architectural historian William Rhoads for their professional wisdom.

We give thanks to Bradley Umble, the project's excellent intern, for the materials he discovered from hours of research and for his design sense and knowledge of electronic media. Eileen Panetta provided valuable insights and support.

We are grateful to Steve Hoare of Black Dome Press for his enthusiasm and expertise. This publication would not be possible without him. Ron Toelke and Barbara Kempler-Toelke have created a handsome book design that melds text and images seamlessly. Ruth Elwell has prepared the all-important index.

The contributors to this publication have broadened our perspective of the period. While many of us have our own memories, their knowledge, range of expertise and point of view will enrich us for years to come. We thank, in addition to guest scholar Roger Panetta, who also assisted with the editing of this volume, Harvey Flad, Gail Godwin and Frances Halsband, Hugh Reynolds, William B. Rhoads, Lowell Thing and George G. Washington.

Susan Farkas has produced a video that is a fascinating and revealing document of this project and, by extension, the IBM era.

Retired IBMers have been the core of our volunteers. A very big thank you goes to Patricia Finch, Friends Board member, for her countless interviews and administration of many aspects of the project, and also to Lowell Thing for his devotion to the oral history project. We are grateful to Dick Coller, whose expert knowledge of the former IBM plant is second to none, to George G. (Jerry) Washington, who devoted hours to compiling a timeline for the IBM plant and associated community developments, to Frank Almquist, Gerald Berke, Frank Brice, Victoria Hanast, Susan LeVangia, Jo Ann Cella, Dick Jones, Gaynel Tavares and John DeJoy. Bruce Whistance's superb photos tell a compelling story of work in the plant and life outside. John F. Matthews's archive of images has proven invaluable. These are only a few of those who offered memories and memorabilia. People from Kingston and the surrounding area who interacted with IBM and IBMers gave us their perspectives, and we thank Kayla Feldman, John Shults, William Davenport, and Jack Finch, among many others.

In all, we conducted oral history interviews with fifty-two individuals, and their memories will provide a lasting record of the IBM years. We thank them all.

Access to materials is the key to organizing a successful exhibition. Jason Cosenza, Ulster Town Clerk, Margie Menard of the Kingston Library and Paul Lasewicz, Bill Bucher and Dawn Stanford from IBM have been indispensable to our efforts. We also wish to thank Lisa Milhaven and Roy Anderson (also a retired IBMer) of the Fair Street Reformed Church for allowing us to gain access to documents related to architect William Van Benschoten. Renée Silver generously donated renderings and other materials produced by her late husband, architect Arthur Silver, for Temple Emanuel in Kingston and the Overlook United Methodist Church in Woodstock. Sandra Hutton allowed access to the materials from architect George Hutton's archive. The staff and members of Temple Emanuel, Congregation Ahavath Israel and St. George's Greek Orthodox Church were welcoming and forthcoming. The Kingston City School District has important holdings from the period, and we thank Friends Board Member and retired Principal Anna Brett, Superintendent Paul Padalino, and Assistant Superintendents MaryStephanie Corsones and Allen Olsen for their help and materials. A thank you to Kyla Haber, Kingston's Assistant Planner, for her help with the city's 1961 Master Plan. We also are grateful to former Friends Board member Marjorie Rovereto; Deborah Medenbach of the *Times Herald-Record*; Walter Maxwell; Don Verity of Pamal Broadcasting; Ira Fusfeld, Robert O'Leary, Diane Zucker-Pineiro, and Tony Adamis of the *Daily Freeman*; Sheldon Martin; Richard Heppner of the Historical Society of Woodstock; Tom Tryniski of fultonhistory.com; and Richard Turck and the members of the "I'm from Kingston" Facebook group. Neil Larson generously shared his research on twentieth-century architecture in the Town of Poughkeepsie. Tessa Killian of the Southeastern New York Library Resources Council provided early and consistent support. We are very grateful for the access to the former IBM Plant, now Tech City, provided by Alan Ginsberg.

If through error we have left your name out, please know that we remain grateful for your contributions.

Ward L.E. Mintz
Exhibition Coordinator

Ward Mintz is the Project Director of Kingston—The IBM Years. *He is a member of the Board of Directors of the Friends of Historic Kingston and has spent his career in the museum field, both as an administrator and curator, and as a staff member at government and foundation supporters of museums in New York State and the region.*

IBM's Early Days in the Hudson Valley: Poughkeepsie and Kingston

By Harvey K. Flad

"IBM's enormous impact on the Poughkeepsie urban region and Kingston during the second half of the twentieth century is hard to overstate."[1]

Introduction

Over the course of the twentieth century, the collection, storage, processing and use of information changed the world. Computers and technology would completely change the way in which Americans viewed their role in the world, in trade, warfare, geopolitics and social discourse.[2] International Business Machines corporation (IBM) emerged as the leader in this economic, military, political and cultural shift.

In the quarter century from 1940 to 1965, the development of the computer as a general tool that would affect all aspects of people's lives emerged through the efforts of many people who lived and worked in the Hudson River Valley of New York State. Research, development and manufacturing by IBM in laboratories and plants in Dutchess and Ulster counties dominated the economic landscape of the region as IBM became a world leader in computer technology.

IBM Poughkeepsie

World War II changed the social landscape of the mid-Hudson Valley. IBM's presence in the Hudson Valley began in 1941 in Poughkeepsie as the Munitions Manufacturing Company. Thomas Watson, Sr., chairman and CEO of IBM from 1914 to 1956, purchased the R. U. Delapenha canning factory south of the city of Poughkeepsie on Route 9 to manufacture military munitions, such as aircraft fire control systems and Browning automatic carbine rifles. A decade later, during the Cold War, IBM would leap from electromechanical punch card calculators to electronic computers and become the prime innovator, designer and manufacturer of the mainframe computer revolution.[3]

Under pressure from the War Department in 1940 to assist the war effort, Watson, Sr. offered President Roosevelt IBM facilities for manufacturing munitions. However, he did not want to use his plant in Endicott. Officers at the Watervliet Arsenal in the Albany area urged that he pick a site along the Hudson River. After conferring with Frederick Hart, owner of a machine shop in Poughkeepsie and an IBM subcontractor, the Route 9 Delapenha campus was purchased. Along with the former canning factory, a new cement-block building known as Plant 001 was constructed and, as the number of employees increased, a cafeteria was added. The campus would continue to expand with the mammoth Building 002 in 1948.[4] Later additions to IBM's impact on the local landscape would include the IBM Country Club across Route 9, a network of research laboratories including Kenyon and Building 701 on Boardman Road, and the leasing of buildings on High Street and elsewhere in the city of Poughkeepsie. Research in these labs would lead directly to IBM's later decision to expand their operations northward across the Hudson River to Kingston, about twenty-eight miles away.

From Calculators to Computers

IBM's shift from electromechanical tabulating machines to electronic computing systems for both business and the military began shortly after World War II. As the Cold War began and tensions between the United States and the Soviet Union escalated, the military sought ways to integrate overall control of its air defense systems to include a computerized network of radar stations in Canada and Alaska known as the DEW (Distant Early Warning) line.

In its March 1953 headline, "We Can Smash the Red A-Bombers," the *Saturday Evening Post* dramatically reported on the anxiety about the possibility of an effective air defense against an atomic bomb attack.[5] The Defense Department and the Eisenhower administration debated the merits of an offensive defense such as deploying bombers of the Strategic Air Command (SAC), versus an as-yet-not-built complex ground radar system. Due to the urgency for an operational defense, the decision was made to combine both approaches. The Soviet hydrogen bomb explosion of 1953 renewed public fear of a nuclear holocaust and this, "combined with the 'can-do' technological mindset of the 1940s and 1950s," generated the momentum for an integrated air defense controlled through computer technology.[6]

Even four years later, during the scramble to build an effective air defense system with the SAGE (Semi-Automatic Ground Environment) computer network, *Time* magazine continued to report the national angst, although offering an optimistic future, as it reported in 1957: "Built over a period of nine years at a cost of more than $18 billion, based on radar networks within networks electronically tied to the most modern systems of detection and interception … it was never considered foolproof against penetration. A defense in depth, it was designed to—and will—limit to a minimum the breakthrough of Soviet long-range bombers coming to pour nuclear destruction on the U.S."[7]

By 1950, Jay Forrester at MIT had begun advanced research on developing a computer, dubbed Whirlwind, that would meet the speed and storage necessary for such a complex system posed by the need for an effective air defense. After numerous meetings between MIT and IBM scientists, IBM was offered a subcontract on October 27, 1952, with MIT's Lincoln Laboratory to proceed with the project.[8] According to Forrester, IBM won the contract over Remington Rand due to its "much higher degree of purposefulness, integration, and esprit de corps and the evidence of much closer ties between research, factory, and field maintenance," as well as a "greater experience in transferring electronic equipment from development to the factory … superior technical ability among key technical staff members, superior field service, and closer proximity to MIT."[9] All of these virtues laid the foundation for IBM's eventual expansion to Kingston where the components of SAGE would be built, tested, and field operators trained.[10]

Meanwhile, IBM had already made efforts to expand its business machines from electromechanical devices to electronic computing systems. Competitors such as Remington Rand's UNIVAC developed large-scale electronic systems for airline record keeping that used magnetic tape storage. In late 1949 and early 1950, IBM began planning for the Tape Processing Machine, or TPM, that was designed and built over the next two years.

During that time frame there would be an effort to advance this commercial supercalculator for scientific purposes; this was originally called the Defense Calculator, and ultimately became the IBM 701.[11] As recalled by Cuthbert C. Hurd, co-manager of the project with Ralph L. Palmer, the name "Defense Calculator" was chosen "to ease some of the internal opposition to it since it could be viewed as a special project (like the bombsights, rifles, etc., IBM had built during World War II) that was not intended to threaten IBM's main product line."[12]

IBM and MIT

The joint contract between MIT and IBM to design and build a supercomputer capable of managing the Early Warning System for the U. S. Defense Department began in earnest in 1952. IBM rented two floors in a former necktie factory on High Street on the north side of the city of Poughkeepsie, where work on the TPM and the Defense Calculator (701) previously had been concentrated. "The third floor of a necktie factory which had previously been used by IBM, was renovated to make room for this project. It was here on High Street that 'Project High' was initially designed."[13] In January 1953 twenty-six engineers moved from the South Road laboratory in Poughkeepsie to the new location on High Street; by August 1954 Project High had 264 employees working at the site.[14] The High Street building posed a number of problems, however. For example, the building was steam heated, and the very dry air caused problems for the electrostatic clutches, so the air valves were removed from the radiators to raise the humidity; this solved the problem until a permanent solution could be made.

The IBM part of the project got its first name, Project High, from this High Street location. The overall project continued to be referenced by the MIT designation of Whirlwind II, but as IBM became more deeply involved, it was clear that a name less closely identified with MIT was needed.

The name SAGE was adopted and remained the description to the end of the project. Begun as a federal project for military defense, it would later be described as one of four "monumental projects that changed the modern world."[15] A revolutionary step, "SAGE marked the first effort to apply computers to large-scale problems of real-time *control*, as distinct from calculation and information processing."[16] As promoted by IBM in their 75th-anniversary edition of *THINK* magazine, "'Real time' data processing arrives in 1958 with the SAGE (Semi-Automatic Ground Environment) computer, built at the Kingston, N.Y. plant for the North American Defense System. Largest of all vacuum tube machines at 113 tons, it was fed information from hundreds of radar sites in the United States, Canada and Iceland."[17]

The single computer system that emerged combined the magnetic core memory of Whirlwind with the calculating speed of IBM 701. IBM engineers had

Cover of an IBM instruction manual for the SAGE computer system, c. 1959. Collection of the Friends of Historic Kingston.

already progressed from the IBM 603, an electromechanical calculator, to the IBM 604, an electronic calculator that used vacuum tubes. By 1952 a group under the leadership of Ralph Palmer developed the IBM 701 with a magnetic tape drive that was capable of 2,200 multiplications a second. As production increased, the demand for greater storage capacity arose, which led to the development of reliable, high-speed ferrite magnetic core memories. Development of the 701 led to expansion of the Kenyon labs on Boardman Road in Poughkeepsie next to Vassar College with the construction of Building 701; ground was broken in April 1953, and the building was dedicated in October 1954. Kenyon House was retrofitted for meeting facilities and visitors. In late 1954 a ferrite core manufacturing facility was established in the South Road plant.

The technology (electronics) and methodology (stored program and automatic control) of the 701 were sharp breaks from IBM's previous technology (punched cards and relays) and previous methodology (control panels and manual operation). The 701 would prove to be one thousand times faster than punched-card equipment, could carry out multiplications indefinitely for all practical purposes, could automatically and instantaneously change from one set of instructions to a completely different set of instructions, and "allowed, for the first time, the automatic processing of hundreds of thousands—and millions and billions—of operations with no human intervention whatsoever."[18]

Demand grew for the 701—IBM's first large-scale, high-speed, stored program electronic computer—from its production in 1953. One year later IBM announced the 702, described as an "Electronic Data Processing Machine" for commercial purposes, with 2,500 cathode-ray tubes and three miles of wire and magnetic tape that could do 7,200 operations per second.

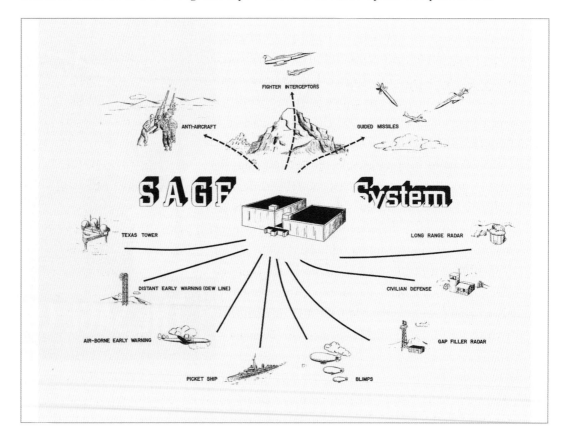

SAGE system diagram. Collection of Friends of Historic Kingston.

Although IBM's primary interest remained in developing and manufacturing business machines, its production of components of the SAGE system established it as the foremost company in the emerging computer industry. Later, in October 1955, the Military Products Division, soon to be renamed the Federal Systems Division, was officially formed and included the Poughkeepsie, Kingston and Owego, New York, plants. As recalled by Jim Bliss, who arrived at the Poughkeepsie plant in 1957 from the Air Force to help develop the Synchronous Transmitter Receiver (STR) for SAGE, the space for Military Products Division work had tight security. "You had to go through two different security check gates," he recalled.

S.A.G.E.

"By almost any measure—scale, expense, technical complexity, or influence on future developments—the single most important computer project of the postwar decade was MIT's Whirlwind and its offspring, the SAGE computerized air defense system," according to history of technology scholar Paul N. Edwards.[19]

SAGE was the heart of the U. S. Air Force's air warning network. It was massive, complex, spread across the country and expensive. In a public relations effort to describe the system at a time of great public fear of an atomic bomb attack, a "Fact Sheet on Project SAGE," distributed by IBM in 1961, reads like an advertisement for a computer war game on an early version of PlayStation:

> It combines the abilities of the world's fastest electronic computer to receive information, to memorize, to calculate and to record answers, with the perspective and display talents of radar to present an instantaneous graphic picture of the location, speed, and direction of all planes within radar range. With a knowledge of flight plans of friendly planes available in the computer, hostile planes can be identified immediately and the most effective defense action taken—again on the basis of computer information and instruction.
>
> The SAGE system starts with a radar ring—on land, on Navy picket ships at sea, on offshore Texas Towers, and on airborne early warning planes ranging far out over the sea. These radars are linked by telephone lines or ultra high frequency radio directly to the high speed computer. Information about aircraft anywhere within the radar area is relayed continuously and automatically to the computer. This IBM-built equipment, called AN/FSQ-7, digests all of this information plus Ground Observer reports, flight plans, and weather information as fast as it is received, and translates it into the over-all picture of the air situation. These TV-like pictures show the air battle as it develops and provides the basis for the necessary human judgments.
>
> The computer automatically calculates for the operator the most effective employment of such defensive weapons as guided missiles, anti-aircraft batteries, and jet interceptors. In the case of the intercepting jets, the aircraft is controlled

Collage of ten photographs of the IBM SAGE Computer. Courtesy of IBM.

The IBM SAGE Computer
Designed, Manufactured, and Installed by IBM for the United States Air Force.

1 radar mappers
2 mapper console
3 operating console
4 command post
5 display console pattern
6 weapons direction
7 magnetic core memory
8 typical computer frames
9 magnetic tape memory
10 magnetic drum memory

by directions fed by radio directly from the computer to the automatic pilot in the plane. Missiles are controlled similarly. At any time, the air battle commander can have the computer display the over-all situation or whatever part of it he wishes to monitor in detail. As the battle moves, information is transferred spontaneously to an adjacent computer.[20]

The early fifties saw the development of proto-types named XD-1 and XD-2 with work at laboratories in Lexington, Massachusetts, and Poughkeepsie and Kingston, New York.[21] In June 1956 the first SAGE computer was shipped to the New York Defense Sector site at McGuire Air Force Base, Wrightstown, New Jersey. After two years of rigid test and program development, this first air defense site began performing its air defense mission on July 1, 1958. On August 7, 1958, a BOMARC missile in Cape Canaveral, Florida, was successfully launched against target drones flying out over the Atlantic and guided by its operator staff engineer Robert E. Ross at the SAGE console in XD-2 at Kingston, 1,500 miles away.[22] Four days after this event, 1,640 personnel moved into the Kingston laboratory.[23]

When completed and deployed to 22 other U.S. sites and one in Canada, SAGE became the largest computer system of its time. Each of the 24 installed machines weighed 250 tons, had two computers and occupied an acre of floor space. The AN/FSQ-7 used a total of 50,000 vacuum tubes and enough electrical power sufficient for a town of several thousand people. Each central processor was capable of driving 100 dis-play consoles, accepting data from 100 on-line operators and 12 remote sites, and providing data to these same sites and more, performing about 75,000 instructions per second for networking regional radars.[24]

Project SAGE was embraced and successfully developed as the primary air defense system for the country. Its reliability, serviceability and operational availability exceeded 99 percent. To achieve these objectives IBM alone, at its peak involvement, had over 7,000 people (almost 20 percent of its workforce) assigned to SAGE in development, manufacturing, maintenance, and other support functions.[25]

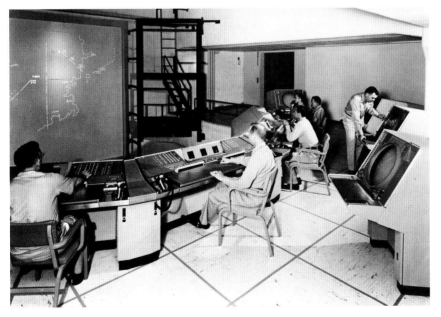

Above left: SAGE display console with IBM engineer operator, 1956. Courtesy of IBM. Above right: SAGE display console and light gun with Air Force airman operator, 1958. Courtesy of IBM. At left: SAGE system operating console with Air Force personnel, 1958. Courtesy of IBM.

Legacy of SAGE

The SAGE project was responsible for many scientific and engineering breakthroughs in computer technology. The very long list includes the following technical advances and inventions: real-time-on-line operation; magnetic core memory; video displays; light guns (now called light pens); the first effective algebraic computer language; graphic display techniques; printed circuit boards; simulation techniques; synchronous parallel logic (digits transmitted simultaneously, rather than serially, through the computer); analog-to-digital and digital-to-analog conversion techniques; digital data transmission over telephone lines; duplexing or doubling of every computer part to guard against system failure; multiprocessing; and networks (automatic data exchange among different computers). "Some, such as networking and graphic displays, comprise the very backbone of modern computing."[26]

Back panel assembly in Kingston plant, 1957. Courtesy of IBM.

As a company, IBM gained both income and technological expertise from its work on SAGE. "IBM built fifty-six SAGE computers at a price of about $30 million apiece; the company's total income from SAGE during the 1950s was about $500 million ... more than half of IBM's income in the 1950s came from military sources."[27] IBM also gained technological knowledge. For example, the 305 RAMAC (random access) storage system became the major form of information storage in computers from the mid-1950s until well into the 1970s. IBM's SABRE airline reservation system, completed in 1964, was the first networked commercial real-time transaction processing system. Its acronym stands for Semi-Automatic Business Research Environment, a direct reference to SAGE (Semi-Automatic Ground Environment), whose essential network structure it copied.

The coordinated project between Lincoln Laboratory and IBM included all phases to design, manufacture, install, and maintain SAGE computers for the nationwide network of air

SAGE computer frames, including IBM and USAF telephone, 1959. Courtesy of IBM.

defense sites. As Robert Crago, assistant manager in 1955 and manager in 1956 of the Kingston plant and laboratory, commented about coordination between IBM and MIT, "It was probably the first experience most of us in IBM had in working with an outside group and taking the leadership from them. … I think the kind of technical camaraderie that grew out of this project made it the most exciting thing that I've ever been involved in."[28] In Poughkeepsie the IBM team of scientists consisting of Steven Dunwell, Werner Bucholz, Harold Ross, N. P. Edwards and a few others worked in limited quarters on High Street.

It had become obvious by 1953 that the project had become much too large for the available space in Poughkeepsie. "Poughkeepsie was full," according to Ray Boedecker, who was responsible for facilities planning at the time and later became general manager of manufacturing and an IBM vice president.[29] IBM already leased space in many small and medium-sized buildings throughout Dutchess County, but for a new enormous factory, comparable to the Poughkeepsie plant, to manufacture its emerging computers and other electronic machines, it sought space across the Hudson River in Ulster County.

IBM's Move to Kingston

In a personal letter from Thomas J. Watson to Fred Eisler dated November 9, 1953, Watson gave "all credit for IBM's decision to locate in Kingston" to his longtime friend.[30] Eisler, owner of the Stuyvesant Hotel in Kingston, and Watson were friends for over forty years, having met while Eisler was senior assistant manager of the Waldorf in New York, where Watson lived with his family. Watson recollected in his November 9 letter that, five years earlier, Eisler had suggested that when IBM needed more facilities it should look at properties in the Kingston area. Watson recalled that after Eisler showed him and William Mair, general manager in Poughkeepsie, several properties in Kingston, Watson had told Eisler "several times that when we were ready to expand we had Kingston at the head of our list."[31] Eisler's letter in response the next day—to "T. J."—said it was his "dream come true" and that "it is the talk of the town, and everyone is so really excited over IBM coming to Kingston."[32]

On November 7, 1953, Thomas J. Watson, Sr. announced that a plant would be built in Kingston. Watson, as chairman of the board, and other IBM officials—

William J. Mair and Dause L. Bibby—announced their plans to local businessmen and political leaders, including: Myron Boice; Bertram Burns, editor *Saugerties Daily Post*; George J. Kaufman, former Judge Surrogate of Ulster County; Alva S. Staples, president Kingston Trust Co.; Charles G. Murray, managing editor *Poughkeepsie New Yorker*; Pratt Boice, president Ulster County Savings Bank; and Percy Bush, supervisor of the Town of Ulster.[33] In February 1954, IBM purchased Boice's Dairy Farm, 200 acres on the outskirts of the city of Kingston. Ground was broken for site construction in May.

In the meantime IBM leased a bowling alley to manufacture sub-assemblies for SAGE systems. On April 9, 1954, the *Poughkeepsie New Yorker* reported:

International Business Machines Corp. made known today that operations will begin Monday in the rented facilities at 23–27 Grand Street, Kingston, formerly known as the 'Bowlatorium.' Approximately 40 persons will be employed initially at this location. They are residents of Kingston and vicinity, who have been

Ruzzo Bowlatorium, 1954. Courtesy of IBM.

employed at the Poughkeepsie plant for some time. They will be engaged in work on a government contract of a restricted nature. This Kingston site was rented pending the construction of the new Ulster county plant north of Kingston. The building contains approximately 30,000 square feet on one floor. Structural changes have been made in the building which formerly housed bowling alleys and a restaurant. It is expected that the work force there will grow to 175 by the end of the year. This group will be made up largely of Kingston residents presently employed at the Poughkeepsie plant. Employment and procurement activity will continue to be handled at Poughkeepsie. Irving P. Maurer, who will be in charge of the group, is a native of Port Ewen and has been employed by IBM for six years.

IBM has completed plans to establish factory facilities in an area of more than 200 acres of land north of Kingston and east of the State Thruway. The site of the factory is within a mile of the Thruway interchange, north of Kingston city limits, and borders the West Shore railroad. It is within a short distance of Route 9-W and also is close to the route of the approach highway to the projected Kingston-Rhinecliff bridge.[34]

In the early 1950s Kingston's location with respect to transportation had improved significantly. As IBM began its move to Kingston, the New York State Thruway (I-87) neared completion—the Ulster County section in 1954–55, and the final segment from Yonkers to the Bronx in summer 1956. Also, preliminary construction had begun in 1954 of the Kingston-Rhinecliff Bridge across the Hudson River.[35]

Following the announcement in 1953 that IBM would build a plant in Kingston about two miles north of the city line in the Town of Ulster, many officials and businessmen from the Kingston area were invited to a dinner at the Poughkeepsie Country Club to meet and "get acquainted with the organization [so that] city and town officials in areas adjacent to the plant were assured that everything would be done to establish cooperation regarding mutual problems."[36] Over the next few months, prior to breaking ground for the plant in early 1954, numerous issues were raised and resolved. For example, the city of Kingston agreed to provide an adequate water supply. Traffic was a concern since the New York Thruway was close to completion, construction of the Rhinecliff-Kingston Bridge was underway (it opened to New York State Route 199 traffic in February 1957), and a Route 9W arterial, town access roads and a bypass were under construction. Attention was also paid to population growth with respect to housing and school enrollments. Housing subdivisions and new schools would ensue in the surrounding towns over the next few years.

Turner-Campbell Construction of New York and Poughkeepsie oversaw construction of the IBM Kingston project. In an effort to include subcontractors and vendors from the area, nine of the seventy-seven subcontractors were from Kingston and three were from Poughkeepsie. The nine from Kingston included: J. A. Cassidy & Son for miscellaneous sheet metal work; Central Hudson Gas & Electric for site electrical lines; the Hutton Company for common bricks; Island Dock Lumber Company for masonry cement and sand materials; John H. Matthews for plumbing

Overhead view of architect drawing of Kingston plant, planned for IBM's Military Products and Electric Typewriter Divisions. Architects, Giffels and Vallet, Inc. and L. Rossetti, Detroit, Michigan. Courtesy of IBM.

of the truck dock; Miron Building Products Company for form lumber; New York Telephone Co. for site telephone lines; Ready Mixed Concrete, Inc. for concrete; and Luke H. Sheeley Sons for plumbing in the boiler house. The three firms from Poughkeepsie were: V. J. Costanzi, Inc. for rental of excavation equipment; Fairview Building Block Company for masonry blocks; and Windsor Building Supplies Corp. for glass blocks and accessories.[37]

In February 1955 the first product engineering group moved to Kingston. By mid-year approximately 900 employees had been relocated from Poughkeepsie locations, and in October 1955 the Military Products Division was officially formed.[38]

By 1956 IBM had already set up a housing department to assist workers seeking housing, both temporary, such as the field engineering students who would move to

their various SAGE sites upon completion of their training, and more permanent housing for engineers, scientists and factory workers on the various projects. Initially, IBM placed advertisements in area newspapers for listings of available rentals; later the company worked with area realtors. Eventually, separate housing departments operating in the autonomous divisions assisted their workers with information on realtors and rental agents. For example, Giles Rittenberry joined IBM in September 1957 as an engineer in testing circuit boards and frames. With assistance on housing from his division, he first rented an apartment on Main Street and later purchased a house on Plymouth Avenue. Edmund J. O'Reilly, a realtor in Kingston, was engaged by IBM in early 1955 to determine whether houses and rental units were available and ready for occupancy. However, the program began slowly in some divisions. As reported later that year, although the housing list was to be available for all employees, "it is apparent that our employees below the management level are not properly informed of the existence of such a list."[39]

In moving to Kingston, the need for space in close proximity to the Poughkeepsie labs was most significant. As Watson, Jr. made clear in his remarks at the dedication of the main plant on November 2, 1956, Fred Eisler "kept barraging Dad with letters about what a fine place this would be for a plant." Watson continued, "And at long last, we came over and looked at it, and it was close to Poughkeepsie, and at that time we thought we would make typewriters here. So we started in Kingston for that reason, and the typewriter has outgrown their part of the facilities, and before very long this will be a sole Military Products Plant."[40]

Manufacturing SAGE components, Kingston plant, 1959. Courtesy of IBM.

Meanwhile, an expanding labor force to manufacture and assemble parts of the SAGE system was also a factor. By January 1, 1956, 670 IBM professional, technical, and administrative persons were involved in SAGE development, plus an additional 817 involved in manufacturing. Nine months later there were 5,268 employees working in Kingston in both the Electric Typewriter and Military Products divisions: 2,244 in the Electric Typewriter Division, of which 1,983 were in manufacturing; and 3,024 in the Military Products Division, of which 1,979 were in manufacturing.

SAGE components began to be assembled, as a description of a photograph of a female worker in the *IBM Kingston News* in early 1956 headlines: "U. S. Defense—and the Hands of a Woman: Within this frame [of circuits] her delicate touch seals hundreds of parts, and the

SAGE core panel assembly, Kingston plant, 1959. Courtesy of IBM.

Engineer's plan for SAGE moves toward reality."[41] "Autofab," an automatic assembly machine, sped up production of partial circuit card assemblies, adding resistors, capacitors, pulse transformers and diodes.

Between 1955 and 1956, the first SAGE shipment, the beginning of commercial manufacturing with the first shipment of typewriters, and continued construction of the main plant on Neighborhood Road and Boices Lane occupied IBM Kingston.[42]

Kingston officials, businessmen and citizens welcomed the opening of the main plant on November 2, 1956. The company invited the public to the dedication ceremonies and an open house to tour the plant.

Thomas J. Watson, Jr. dedicated the Kingston plant at a luncheon attended by air force personnel, business and civic leaders of the community, and IBM executives. C. F. McElwain, general manager IBM Military Products Division, presided over the ceremonies. Speakers included Lieutenant General Donald L. Putt, chief of staff for development, United States Air Force, and Dr.

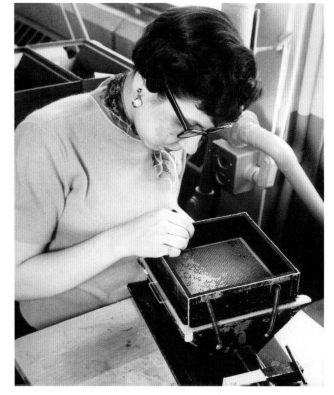

Woman working on core assembly. Courtesy of the John F. Matthews Collection.

James R. Killian, president of Massachusetts Institute of Technology. Mayor Frederick H. Stang and Kingston Chamber of Commerce President George J. Silkworth welcomed the company to the community. Harold L. Felton, chairman of the Kingston IBM advisory board, assisted in laying the cornerstone. "Following the ceremonies, guests were conducted through the manufacturing facilities for the SAGE computer and IBM electric typewriters." The next day the plant was open "for inspection by IBM employees, their families, and all interested area residents."[43]

Over 40,000 residents attended the open house. The *Kingston Daily Freeman* devoted two full sections to the occasion, and a special run of the *Saugerties Daily Post* included dozens of congratulatory advertisements and statements from area businesses. Corporate IBM responded in kind as Thomas Watson, Sr. personally sent letters of appreciation thanking each of the individuals and groups.[44]

As described years later by IBM's Department of Information, "When the Kingston plant was dedicated on November 2, 1956, a plant of 747,190 square feet, a 40,000 square-foot warehouse, a power plant and waste treatment plant had arisen from an Ulster County cornfield. During the next two years, a 132,000 square-foot engineering research laboratory was added."[45] In August 1958 1,640 employees moved into the newly completed laboratory building. The next year work began on the Strategic Air Command Control System (SACCS), and in 1960 Kingston lab was awarded a contract for a Project Mercury subsystem. IBM renamed its Military Division as the Federal Systems Division (FSD) and designated Kingston as the IBM Command Control Center.

Image composed of interior view of IBM Kingston engineering lab with two engineers and view of main plant façade in background, 1958. Courtesy of IBM.

IBM remained committed to business and commercial data processing, and Kingston joined the Data Systems Division in January 1962. Some of the IBM commercial data processing machine assemblies that it produced, such as for typewriters, included automatic carriages, plate counters, brush blocks, ratchet counters, paper compartments, type wheels, comb bars and jumper wires.

IBM electric typewriters nearing the end of the two-mile-long assembly line in the Kingston plant, c. 1956. Courtesy of IBM.

Electric typewriters had been manufactured in Poughkeepsie since the 1950s. In 1956, Kingston IBM built a new plant, "the first new factory in the world designed solely for the manufacture of electric typewriters." The "gradual move from Poughkeepsie to Kingston" of men and women workers along with 350 tons of equipment "the 28-mile distance from plant to plant" was accomplished over several weekends that spring.[46] Four different IBM electric typewriters were manufac-

tured: the basic electric; executive model; one with decimal tabulation keys; and the Formswriter.

IBM's commercial products manufactured in Kingston were significant exports of the company, and access to the newly constructed New York State Thruway had become an important factor in the location of the campus. During the 1960s IBM's advanced computer systems from SAGE to SABRE to Stretch to IBM 360/systems maintained a large workforce at the Kingston campus.

The Kingston IBM Community

Newsletters offered employees in all divisions information on health benefits and payroll check procedures, as well as informing them of the opening of the country club and the swimming pool, and numerous other recreational and professional activities such as continuing education seminars. Most activities were held on site, although some events were off site. For example, on November 28, 1956, a "classified" engineering seminar on the BOMARC weapon and integration with SAGE was held at the Research Laboratory Auditorium in Poughkeepsie for employees in the Military Products Division, although "limited to those with secret clearance."[47]

News about individual hires and promotions helped to establish an IBM sense of community and corporate identity, while company-sponsored programs encouraged family allegiance to the firm. For example, in January 1956 there was a public showing of "SAGE," a film for the employees of the Kingston Military Products Division and their families that promoted the division's role in the defense of the country.[48] Along with the showing of the film was a talk by G.A. Cullen, Kingston IBM general manager, and R.P. Crago, assistant general manager. The film was shown at both the IBM Country Club in Poughkeepsie and at the Community Theatre in Kingston.

Managers and other employees quickly became involved in local nonprofit and charitable organizations.[49] Managers were elected to directorates of the Kingston Area Chamber of Commerce, the City of Kingston Hospital, and the Benedictine Hospital in Kingston. The company made donations to the hospitals' capital funds for new building expansion. As in other IBM sites such as Poughkeepsie, many employees became active in a variety of civic institutions and local organizations.

1960s–1980s

Along with Poughkeepsie, Kingston labs and manufacturing cooperated in developing more complex machines with greater calculating speed and storage capacity. By 1959 transistors were replacing vacuum tubes. When Earl Buton, who had joined IBM right out of an electrical engineering degree from Ohio State University in 1954, returned from two years in the air force, he began working on transistor circuit design in Building 201, just behind the main building on the Kingston campus.

Transistors were being developed by Bell Labs in the late 1950s, and IBM saw them as a way to overcome issues inherent in current circuitry. As transistors became smaller and smaller, Buton worked to integrate them into the computer systems that were rapidly emerging from the Poughkeepsie and Kingston labs. By 1959 transistors had replaced vacuum tubes, and the IBM 7090 became the first fully transistorized mainframe, capable of 229,000 calculations per second.

By the late 1950s IBM manufactured and sold eight different computers for both the scientific and business communities. Six of them were incompatible and could not communicate with each other. To resolve the problem Steven "Red" Dunwell, deemed by one company historian as its greatest product engineer, came from IBM headquarters in New York City to Poughkeepsie.

In 1956 Dunwell, Werner Bucholz, Gene Amdahl and a few others had undertaken a project to develop a system powerful enough to provide a common architecture for an entire line of computers, called STRETCH. The name was chosen because it "stretched" all of the then-known limits in computers. Stretch was IBM's first transistorized computer and used 170,000 transistors. Although its projected computing power of one hundred times the speed of its 701 computer was never realized, it nevertheless formed the basis for the rest of IBM's line of computers, including the 7090 and System/360.

When completed, Stretch (also known as IBM 7030) was manufactured in Kingston, and the first two Stretch systems were shipped in 1961 from Kingston to the Atomic Energy Commission laboratories in Los Alamos and Lawrence Radiation Laboratory in Livermore, California. A third system, known as IBM 7950 Harvest, was shipped to the National Security Agency in 1962.

Stretch costs were so high that IBM lost millions, and Dunwell was reassigned to IBM's research center at Yorktown Heights, but Tom Watson, Jr. would later apologize and confer an IBM Fellowship upon him.

The IBM 7090 was completed during the same time frame and used a large amount of the technology, processes, and procedures that had been developed and implemented by Stretch. Much as the SAGE system had developed to complement SAC's air defense against an impending Soviet bomber attack, the 7090 was produced for the Ballistic Missile Early Warning System (BMEWS) to intercept Russian ICBMs. The first two transistorized computers were delivered to BMEWS in November 1959 and, by 1961, three tracking stations were operational in Thule, Greenland, Alaska, and the United Kingdom. Jerry Greenberg, who worked on the project from 1959–66, recalled the false alarm on October 5, 1960, when the Thule base radar detected a strong signal implicating an incoming missile from over the North Pole.[50] In fact it was a return signal from the rising moon. However, since there was no comparable signal from a second radar line, the computer never generated an impact prediction, so the SAC commander in the air did not activate any anti-missiles.

A number of advances in computer technology arose from work on the 7090 in Kingston. For example, the Federal Systems Division (formerly MPD) developed a high-speed, high-capacity device called the "Kingston drum" to supplement the system's disk memory. Originally for use on the real-time 7090s used to support NASA's Project Mercury, the Kingston drum was also attached to 7090 computers in the SABRE business product line developed to handle reservations and seat inventory for American Airlines.[51]

Graphic design technology was among the many advances spurred by the developments of IBM machines 709, 7090, and System/360. Project GEM began in the Kingston labs to create a Graphic Expression Machine that could display drawings to automate automobile construction. IBM staff worked with staff from General Motors research laboratory in Warren, Michigan, and the first computers in design automation, named IBM 2250, were shipped to GM in 1962. Automobile hoods and shapes could be mathematically configured using Elmer Sharp's digital design programs from his work in Kingston.[52]

In 1961 more than 5,000 IBMers worked in Kingston under the direction of Richard J. Whalen, general manager, and Harold D. Ross, manager of research and engineering. In addition to the plant population, more than 1,880 field engineers had graduated from the field engineering education course in SAGE computer installation and maintenance and were on duty at SAGE sites throughout North America.

Facilities at Kingston in 1961 included high-power electron microscopes, vacuum metal evaporators for advanced memory component research, a radio interference laboratory for system communication studies, an environmental laboratory for testing components and assemblies, a controlled atmosphere laboratory to eliminate foreign particles, and two IBM 704 computers for administrative, research and engineering operations. In early 1962 Kingston began manufacturing the commercial computers 704/7044.

Meanwhile, in Poughkeepsie, IBM added buildings to its campus on Boardman Road, including buildings 701, 703, and 704. The latter, built as the IBM acoustics lab in 1961 after

acoustical engineer Bill Lang arrived, contains two enormous anechoic chambers and a reverberation room for testing noise levels in all machines. The lab is still in operation even after IBM disposed of its other properties on the campus.

System/360

From 1961–63, as the SAGE project began to wind down in Kingston, IBM rushed to develop the components for System/360. The Stretch project had formed the basic architecture for System/360 that required mass production of transistors. IBM decided to manufacture their own transistors and built a new plant in southern Dutchess County in East Fishkill. Similar to the impact that IBM's growth in the Poughkeepsie area had on housing, commercial and retail business, the construction of the East Fishkill facility and subsequent increase in employees had a significant impact on southern Dutchess County,

including the expansion of a well-educated and well-paid population, housing subdivisions, and shopping malls.[53]

Ulster County's development was equally influenced by IBM's growth. Housing, commercial and retail businesses all expanded, and transportation infrastructure changed the face of the landscape.

On October 25, 1963, the Kingston laboratory went commercial. The lab was transferred from the Federal Systems Division to the Data Systems Division. As space opened up in Kingston with the wind down of SAGE, many of the components to System/360 were manufactured, assembled and shipped from there, such as Models 65, 67 and 75, the IBM 2250 graphics display unit, and power products development. Tom Watson, Jr. introduced System/360 on April 7, 1964, as "the most important product announcement in company history" and described it as "the first large 'family' of computers to use the same software and peripheral equipment."[54]

Thomas J. Watson, Jr. visit to the Kingston plant, 1958. Courtesy of IBM.

System/360 was hugely successful and brought about increased engineering effort and a substantial build-up in the manufacturing responsibilities of the Kingston operations.[55] Three of the models and three other components—power supplies, core memories and cables used on all other models—were engineered and manufactured in the Kingston plant. The IBM 2250 display unit was applied to simulated flight of the Gemini mission, and the one thousandth IBM 2260 was shipped from Kingston. In 1966 plans were made to construct a new building adjacent to the existing building to meet increasing space needs. An 80,000-square-foot warehouse was also built. Over the next two decades there was more construction on the Kingston campus, including various warehouses, Building 202 as a 250,000-square-foot four-story lab, and numerous other buildings for manufacturing and service functions. In

1970 the Kingston laboratory became dedicated to the development of communication systems and produced a number of computer systems, including the IBM 3270 Information Display System, IBM 3600 Finance Communications System and IBM 3790 Communication System, for a wide variety of industry applications. In 1974 Kingston shipped the one hundred thousandth 3270.

The "Great Downsizing"

In 1985, IBM Kingston was at its peak employment total of 7,100. Kingston, Poughkeepsie and East Fishkill reached a maximum employment of 35,000 in 1990, with Kingston's share at that time reduced to 5,700.[56] A year and a half later, on March 30, 1993, the "Great Downsizing" in the mid-Hudson Valley began. "Layoffs begin at IBM," headlined the *Daily Freeman*.[57] Layoffs began at East Fishkill and continued at Kingston and Poughkeepsie. As reported in the story, "IBM began informing managers … that they were 'surplus,' a plant spokesman [in East Fishkill] said." Employees at Kingston and Poughkeepsie were next, to total an elimination of 6,000 of its 21,500 positions at the local sites. Over the next few days 1,200 workers at the Technology Products site in East Fishkill had been let go, with another 2,800 "expected to leave voluntarily."

At the end of 1993, IBM employed 15,500 people in the Hudson Valley, down from 21,600 at the end of 1992. As of December 31 of that year, IBM employed 4,300 people in Kingston, 8,100 in Poughkeepsie, and 9,200 in East Fishkill. Cuts were made in the Enterprise system in both Kingston and Poughkeepsie. "Cuts in the mainframe division were made at every level— from designers to technical workers to engineers— and included both new and longtime workers, said IBM Kingston spokesman Stephen Cole."[58] Counseling centers opened in IBM Building 935 on Boice's Lane Extension in the town of Ulster, the Arnoff building on Neptune Road in Poughkeepsie and the Barney Building near the Mid-Hudson Civic Center in Poughkeepsie.

Kingston Plant Closing

In a Corporate News Bulletin (July 27, 1994): "IBM announced that it will discontinue operations at its Kingston, N.Y. site by year-end 1995, and transfer the 1,500 Kingston employees to Poughkeepsie. No layoffs are associated with this announcement."[59]

According to IBM headquarters, "The decision was made on July 25 by Nicholas M. Donofrio, IBM senior vice president and general manager, Large Scale Computing Division, and his senior executive team. … [They] found that sufficient space and capacity exists in Poughkeepsie to accommodate the manufacturing and development activities now conducted in Kingston. … The move is part of IBM's continuing effort to make its large-scale computing products more competitive by reducing costs. The company expects that, after it dis-

continues operations in Kingston, aggregate, annual savings will approximate $18 million."[60]

IBM pursued a variety of options for the sale or lease of its Kingston property, noted the news bulletin, even as it acknowledged that the closure would have implications for many employees. "We intend to be as innovative as we can in terms of work arrangement flexibility," Donofrio said. "I anticipate that specific organizations will pursue creative approaches to help employees."[61] Donofrio also said the company would take steps to assist the Kingston community and named Stephen W. Cole, mid-Hudson Valley external programs manager, as IBM's liaison to help the community adjust during the transition.

IBM's profitability was foremost. "Our objective in closing Kingston is to increase our ability to compete," Donofrio said, and added, "Consolidating our operations in Poughkeepsie will help us stay profitable. The logic behind our decision is compelling, but logic can't reconcile the mixed emotions we all feel about leaving a community that's been so closely identified with our business over the years, and where our employees have found such a warm welcome. Logic says we can't continue to operate two sites and be as competitive as we must be, but our history and hearts move us to wish otherwise."[62]

"Logic?" Logic for Tom Watson, Sr. reflected patriotism as well as business. Logic for Jay Forrester on the decision for MIT to subcontract the Whirlwind/SAGE project to IBM in 1952 combined spatial and intellectual motives—Poughkeepsie's proximity to Boston, the design and manufacturing expertise of the company, and the esprit de corps of its employees. Logic for Tom Watson, Jr. included invention, creativity, and business growth. Logic for IBM Poughkeepsie's expansion to Kingston was the need for space to assemble, manufacture, test and ship many of its products including SAGE and System/360. Logic for Lou Gerstner's IBM in the early 1990s meant profitability. Although IBM maintained its prominence in the computer industry, it no longer was "family."

"Golden Years"

On the inside of the cover of *14K Days: A History of the Poughkeepsie Laboratory* is a remarkable admission: the forty years from 1944 to 1984 were the "golden years" of IBM Poughkeepsie. The same phrase, albeit for a shorter time of thirty years, can be said for IBM Kingston. Their celebration occurred in 1989 during the corporation's 75th anniversary. IBM Kingston organized a "Heritage Center" that displayed artifacts, photographs, wall texts and a videotape that offered a look at the products made in Kingston that were "directly linked to Kingston's first mission in the 1950s—SAGE."[63] The video featured 1950s footage of a Kingston SAGE computer firing a BOMARC missile during a test exercise. Hundreds of employees, employee families and Kingstonians visited the displays at the center and could also reflect on the many other products manufactured at the Kingston plant.

Former IBMers who reflect on their lives and work in both Poughkeepsie and Kingston during those "golden years" describe their experience in similar terms. Incomes and benefits were good, intellectual discourse was enlightening, and social perks many. IBM families had full use of IBM-furnished swimming pools, picnics, and a golf course. Many traveled to Europe or Asia on IBM business or on holiday. Female workers were given opportunities to advance their careers in an age of gender discrimination, and most employees were offered continuing education to improve their technical skills. IBM encouraged civic engagement and donated sums to nonprofit organizations in which their employees were active. However, it would not last as a new corporate culture emerged. The sale of the Kingston campus is just the most visible result. ⊙

Harvey K. Flad is Emeritus Professor of Geography at Vassar College in Poughkeepsie, New York. Dr. Flad's scholarship has focused on cultural and historic landscapes, artists of the Hudson River School, and environmental and urban planning, including open space preservation and urban revitalization. He is coauthor with social historian Clyde Griffen of Main Street to Mainframes: Landscape and Social Change in Poughkeepsie *(Albany: SUNY Press, 2009).*

Acknowledgments: James Bliss; Ray Boedecker; Earl Buton; Frank Carbin; Mary Flad; Jerry Greenberg; Clyde Griffen; Steve Hoare; Betsy Kopstein, Dutchess County Historical Society; William Lang; Lynn Lucas, Adriance Memorial Library; Ward Mintz; William Rhoads; Giles Rittenberry; Elmer Sharp; Dawn Stanford, IBM Corporate Archives.

Notes

1 Harvey K. Flad and Clyde Griffen, *Main Street to Mainframes: Landscape and Social Change in Poughkeepsie* (Albany: The State University of New York Press, 2009), 171.

2 For a history of computers' influence on society, see Charles & Ray Eames, *A Computer Perspective*, edited by Glen Fleck (Cambridge, MA: The MIT Press, 1973), especially the Introduction by I. Bernard Cohen; Paul N. Edwards, *The Closed World: Computers and the Politics of Discourse in Cold War America* (Cambridge, MA: The MIT Press, 1997).

3 Jeffrey R. Yost, editor, *The IBM Century: Creating the IT Revolution* (Los Alamitos, CA: IEEE Computer Society, 2011); Emerson W. Pugh, *Memories That Shaped an Industry* (Cambridge, MA: The MIT Press, 1984); Charles J. Bashe, Lyle R. Johnson, John H. Palmer, and Emerson W. Pugh, *IBM's Early Computers* (Cambridge, MA: The MIT Press, 1986); Franklin M. Fisher, James W. McKie, and Richard B. Mancke, *IBM and the U.S. Data Processing Industry: An Economic History* (New York: Praeger, 1983); for IBM's presentation see *IBM: A Special Company* (75th Anniversary ed.), *Think*, September 1989.

4 *14K Days: A History of the Poughkeepsie Laboratory* (IBM, 1984); Flad and Griffen, 2009, chapters 10, 11 and 16.

5 Ralph E. Lapp and Stewart Alsop, "We Can Smash the Red A-Bomber," *Saturday Evening Post*, vol. 225, no. 38, March 21, 1953, p. 19.

6 Edwards, 1997, p. 95.

7 *Time*, vol. 80, no. 22, November 25, 1957, p. 58.

8 "From the Beginning," *IBM Lab News*, Kingston, New York, June 12, 1974, p. 1.

9 Pugh, 1984, p. 94; Thomas P. Hughes, *Rescuing Prometheus* (New York: Pantheon Books, 1998), p. 49.

10 Hughes, 1998, chapter 2; Pugh, 1984, chapter 4.

11 Bashe, et.al., 1986, pp. 130–36.

12 Cuthbert C. Hurd, "Early IBM Computers: Edited Testimony," in Yost, 2011, p. 76.

13 *14K Days*, 1984, pp. 7–11; Bashe, et.al., 1986, p. 243.

14 "From the Beginning," 1974, p. 1.

15 Hughes, 1998, p. 16.

16 Paul N. Edwards, "The World in a Machine: Origins and Impacts of Early Computerized Global Systems Models," in Agatha C. Hughes and Thomas P. Hughes, eds., *Systems, Experts, and Computers: The Systems Approach in Management and Engineering, World War II and After* (Cambridge, MA: The MIT Press, 2000), p. 229.

17 *IBM: A Special Company*, 1989, p. 41.

18 Hurd in Yost, 2011, p. 77.

19 Edwards, 1997, p. 75.

20 *Fact Sheet on Project SAGE* (IBM, October 10, 1961).

21 "XD-2, Kingston MPD in Promise, Substance," *IBM News*, May 11, 1956, vol.1, no.11, p. 1.; "From the Beginning," 1974, p. 1; "1957 Engineering Accomplishment Report," Military Products Division, IBM Kingston, 1957 (THP Master Files, IBM Corporate Archives).

22 Hughes, 1998, p. 65; "From the Beginning," 1974, pp. 1–2.

23 "From the Beginning," p. 1.

24 Bashe, et.al., 1986, p. 244.

25 Bashe, et.al., 1986, pp. 244–45.

26 Edwards, 1997, p. 100; Fisher, et.al., 1983, p. 29; Bashe, et.al.1986, p. 244.

27 Edwards, 1997, pp. 101–102.

28 R. P. Crago, 1983, quoted in Bashe, et.al., 1986, p. 244.

29 Ray Boedecker, interview, December 30, 2013.

30 Thomas J. Watson, Sr., letter to Fred Eisler, November 9, 1953, in Thomas J. Watson, Sr. papers, IBM Corporate Archives, thanks to Dawn Stanford, research archivist. Reported in *Kingston Daily Freeman*, "Watson credits Fred Eisler with IBM locating in area—personal letter tells story of efforts by longtime friend," November 10, 1953.

31 Watson, Sr., 1953, ibid.; also referenced by Thomas J.

Watson, Jr. in his remarks on laying the cornerstone of the main plant and the accompanying plaque during dedication ceremonies, November 2, 1956—"In 1948, Mr. Eisler originally talked to my Father about the possibilities of IBM coming to Kingston and later, Mr. Eisler was kind enough to show my Father the area." In "Suggested Outline for Kingston," Thomas J. Watson, Jr. papers, IBM Corporate Archives. For information on William Mair, see Flad and Griffen, 2009, pp. 177–78.

32 Fred J. Eisler, letter to Thomas J. Watson, Sr., November 10, 1953, in Thomas J. Watson, Sr. papers, IBM Corporate Archives; additional letters of thanks to Watson from Harold Keller, New York State Commissioner of Commerce, the Ulster County Board of Supervisors, and Sister M. Perenice, administrator of Benedictine Hospital.

33 "Men Who Helped in IBM's Selection of Local Site," *Kingston Daily Freeman*, November 10, 1953.

34 "IBM to Open Kingston Plant; 40 Begin Work Monday," *Poughkeepsie New Yorker*, April 9, 1954, p. 1.

35 See William Rhoads's essay in this volume, p. 116.

36 J. F. Schuehler, memo to H. T. Rowe, 5 KGN NY 12-10-56, p. 1.

37 J. J. Heller, project engineer, letter to T. J. Liguore at IBM Kingston, n.d., 7 pp.

38 *News for IBM Editors*, November 17, 1959, p. 2.

39 *Kingston Daily Plant Newsletter*, August 29, 1955; O'Reilly had been hired in May, *Kingston Daily Plant Newsletter*, May 18, 1955.

40 Thomas J. Watson, Jr., remarks at dedication November 2, 1956, typescript Belt 7-A, Thomas J. Watson, Jr. papers, IBM Corporate Archives.

41 *IBM Kingston News*, March 23, 1956, vol. 1, no. 8, p. 1.

42 *IBM Kingston News*, March 9, 1956, vol. 1, no. 7; also, IBM Poughkeepsie noted: "The prototype was shipped in January 1955. Twenty-seven subsequent units were manufactured in Kingston, where most of IBM's military contracts were done," *14K DAYS*, 1984, p.11.

43 H.T. Rowe, "IBM Dedicates Kingston Plant," news release, International Business Machines Corp., New York, November 2, 1956.

44 Gavin A. Cullen, plant manager Kingston, letter to D.W. Burns, editor and general manager of the *Saugerties Daily Post*, July 7, 1955, and letter from William W. Ward, office of Thomas J. Watson to G. A. Cullen, plant manager Kingston, August 5, 1955.

45 "The IBM Kingston Story," *News for IBM Editors*, November 12, 1959, p. 3.

46 *IBM Kingston News*, April 27, 1956, vol. 1, no. 10.

47 *Kingston Daily Plant Newsletter*, no. 66, November 28, 1956.

48 *Kingston Daily Plant Newsletter*, January 11, 1956.

49 J. F. Schuehler to H.T. Rowe, Director of Information at World Headquarters in New York City, memo 5 KGN NY 12-10-56.

50 Jerry Greenberg, interview, January 20, 2014; also see "The Moon as a Soviet Missile Attack," a blog by Curtis Simpson.

51 Robert V. Head, "Getting Sabre off the Ground," in Yost, 2011, p. 153.

52 Elmer Sharp, "Digital Design of Contoured Forms," manuscript, April 16, 1963; see also IBM's initial proposal *Project GEM: The Graphic Expression Machine*, July 8, 1960.

53 Flad and Griffen, 2009, pp. 101–206.

54 *IBM: A Special Company*, 1989, p. 51; Flad and Griffen, 2009, pp. 191–193; see also Bob O. Evans, "System/360: a Retrospective View," in Yost, 2011, pp. 173–197.

55 "IBM Expanding in Kingston; Plans Manufacturing Building," *Poughkeepsie Journal*, March 23, 1966, p. 1.

56 *Kingston Daily Freeman*, November 27, 1991.

57 *Kingston Daily Freeman*, March 30, 1993.

58 *Kingston Daily Freeman*, March 31, 1993.

59 "IBM Announces Plan to Close Kingston Site," CHQNEWS *Corporate Headquarters Bulletin*, July 27, 1994.

60 Ibid.

61 Ibid.

62 Ibid.

63 *Dimensions*, 16-page large-format brochure, Kingston, NY, April/May 1989; "Golden Years" caption inside cover of *14K Days*, 1984.

IBM and the Modernization of Kingston, New York

By Roger Panetta

In April 1952 a royal motorcade transported Queen Juliana up Broadway, lined with excited Kingstonians, to the Academy Green to place flowers at the statue of Peter Stuyvesant and sign the Visitor's Book at the First Dutch Reformed church reaffirming the Dutch roots of Kingston and its ancient place in the history of New York.[1]

There was much excitement and anticipation of the visit of Queen Juliana of the Netherlands. It seemed fitting indeed that the first visit of a reigning monarch initiate the city's celebration marking the 300th anniversary of the first settlement of Wiltwyck. The city was decorated with Dutch flags, blue and orange bunting on public buildings, and the planting of thousands of tulips, a gift of the Consul General of Holland. Rain forced the official welcome ceremony indoors to the municipal auditorium where her Majesty was greeted by two thousand Kingstonians. The following September would be the 175th anniversary of the establishment of the government of the State of New York.[2]

Two years of planning generated six months of festivities ranging from folk dancing and first settlers days to art shows, and all culminating in an historic pageant with over five hundred costumed citizens marking the highlights of three centuries of Kingston's history. Fifteen historical events recalled the history of the region and the city's recent contributions to the wars of the twentieth century. An Old Home Week invited former residents to return and join in the festivities. This celebration was both a reminder of Kingston's rich historic past and a continuation of the process of historic remembering that had deep roots in this Hudson Valley city.

In 1895, over half a century earlier, Kingston had staged a "Grand Kirmess and Pardon,"

Historic Kingston. Old Senate House, Kingston, New York, built in 1676. Postcard 1908.

OLD SENATE HOUSE
ERECTED 1676
KINGSTON, N.Y.

a romanticized version of imagined colonial Kingston organized by Lila Stewart.[3] Historic commemorations in 1907 and 1909, the Hudson-Fulton celebrations, marked the beginnings of the new century that would witness the slow but persistent erosion of Kingston's economy. The decline of the extractive industries, including bricks, cement, bluestone, and ice, the obsolescence of the D&H Canal, and the uncompetitive regional railroad system were signs of a structurally weakened economy. Attempts to enter automobile manufacturing, the migration of light trades from New York City, and the World War I renewal of the maritime industries provided only a temporary respite.

Other events sponsored by the DAR and a series of historical pageants laid the foundation for the "colonialization" of Kingston's past, which was now sanctified and fixed. Much of the rich industrial and maritime history was soon eclipsed by the city's canonization of George Clinton, who offered the pedigree to legitimate this claim

of a glorious colonial past providing, in Alf Evers's words, "a cultural and historic distinction to delight some well informed and discriminating tourists."[4]

This array of historic commemorations distracted the public from Kingston's slowly eroding economy. General Electric's rejection of the city in the 1920s for its new Hudson Valley home in Schenectady compelled the Kingston Chamber of Commerce to underwrite a study to help restore the city's prosperity. None of these early-twentieth-century efforts worked, and Kingston soon confronted the heavy blows of the Depression, war, and the fundamental changes in the post-war economy.[5]

In the face of these demoralizing circumstances, the city increasingly turned inward toward its colonial past to sustain its diminished economy and public morale. The dangers of this posture were an increased isolation and insularity reinforced by the continuous reiteration of its historic past and ultimately supporting the city's legitimacy, self-assurance, and credibility.

Early Prosperity. Rondout Creek looking toward Island Dock. Photograph 1900. Collection of Friends of Historic Kingston.

Death of an Old Factory. United States Lace Curtain Mill, Midtown Kingston. Collection of Friends of Historic Kingston. The mill is being repurposed for artists' housing.

Even the construction of the Governor Clinton Hotel in 1924–26, instigated by the outside consulting firm the General Organization Company to attract businessmen and accommodate the expected "flood" of tourists, was undercut by the later proliferation of regional motels.

Kingston is located on the west shore of the Hudson River, 90 miles north of New York and 52 miles south of Albany, at the juncture of three river valleys—the Wallkill, Esopus, and the Rondout, all part of the transportation network that supported the city's nineteenth-century economy. Kingston's varied land mass contains hills, cliffs, and flat plains. Population is concentrated

New Roads, New Accommodations. Motel 19 at New York State Thruway exit 19, Kingston. Postcard.

in the north central area of the original settlement, south central Rondout Creek, and along Broadway, the connecting link. The principal commercial centers are in the Uptown (Stockade District), Rondout (Downtown), and Broadway (Midtown) sections. Uptown, historically the city's main retail area, had been the regional shopping center until it was displaced by new hubs along the city's arteries and connecting highways. The population in 2010 numbered 23,887 residents living in 9,844 households.

The self-imposed insularity of the first half of the twentieth century was challenged by a series of outside forces that would change Kingston in ways that were unexpected and unplanned. The first and most important of these was the construction of the New York State Thruway. Transportation, which had been so critical to Kingston's early history, providing the infrastructure essential to economic development, was returning in its new modern incarnation—the superhighway. In the place of boats and railroads of the nineteenth century, the automobile and the truck of the modern era would link the interests of the region and the state to the city of Kingston.

The Depression had left New York State with

crumbling highways and poor local roads. Municipalities, short of funds, were unable to rectify these shortcomings, leaving planners to lament the unpreparedness for the new auto-centric post-war world.

New York State's government, anxious about the transition to a peacetime economy, wedded the need for modern highways with the concern for jobs and, especially, economic development. Engineers, experienced in using the tools of government for infrastructure development, proposed a 535-mile New York State Thruway north from New York City to Albany and then west to Buffalo.

The Thruway proposal, supported by Republican Governor Thomas Dewey, recalled the *Futurama* exhibit at the 1939 World's Fair, a utopian vision of the coming automobile age. This vision owed much to the Germans and the Autobahn, the innovative highway designed for speed and regional integration. A corollary commitment was made by the state to build urban arterial highways and rural secondary roads to replace some of the horse-and-buggy paths.[6]

Municipalities lobbied and were on alert about the placement of exits and access points to the Thruway. Communities and cities could be made or broken by these decisions that would of course not only link them to the west, but open their doors to the growing suburban exodus from major cities like New York where businesses and urbanites imagined vast tracts of open farmland ripe for development.

On July 11, 1946, ground was broken for the Thruway with the promise of a new era of prosperity. Construction, which had slowed in the early 1950s, was reignited by a determined effort and new financial and political schemes aimed at the completion of the Thruway by decade's end. The second transportation revolution was now underway with the promise of new commercial relationships and economic development.[7] Some predicted that "whole communities would swell or deflate, often in unpredictable ways."[8] In October 1954 at the dedication of the Kingston interchange, State Assemblyman Wilson promised that "with the inevitable expansion of our industry which will follow today's event we will have a corresponding increase in the demand for new housing. ... Indeed there is not a single local resident ... who will not benefit directly or indirectly from the great public work."[9] The manager of the Central Hudson Power Company described the Thruway, proposed bridges, and new highways as "a Golden Grid which would bring Kingston within an overnight haul of a quarter of the U.S. population."[10]

Kingston and Newburgh proclaimed that "the wrong side of the river would soon become the right side." The chambers of commerce in both cities were inundated with hundreds of inquiries about possible building sites along the Thruway. *The New York Times* reported that several major companies had begun to purchase large parcels, driving land values up from Rockland to Ulster counties. In 1954 in response to the Thruway initiative, the Kingston Common Council approved an arterial system to expedite traffic through Kingston and provide easy access to the Thruway. The city Planning Commission asserted that "it would be of inestimable benefit for a manufacturer to have his product within ninety minutes of 'the' market which is the situation with Kingston on the Thruway."[11]

Albert Kurdt, executive secretary of the Kingston Chamber of Commerce, announced the Thruway had started "an industrial boom ... which will rejuvenate Kingston, its 29,000 people and the whole Hudson valley region."[12] Kingston's chamber of commerce and its planning com-

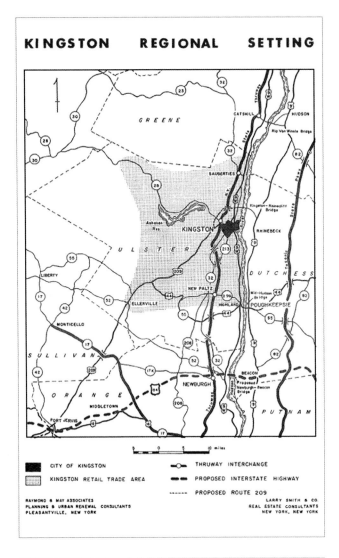

KINGSTON   REGIONAL   SETTING

CITY OF KINGSTON   THRUWAY INTERCHANGE
KINGSTON RETAIL TRADE AREA   PROPOSED INTERSTATE HIGHWAY
                                PROPOSED ROUTE 209

RAYMOND & MAY ASSOCIATES   LARRY SMITH & CO.
PLANNING & URBAN RENEWAL CONSULTANTS   REAL ESTATE CONSULTANTS
PLEASANTVILLE, NEW YORK   NEW YORK, NEW YORK

Kingston's Strategic Location. Kingston Comprehensive Development Plan, Raymond and May and Associates, 1961. Courtesy of City of Kingston Planning Department.

defined as places where high-tech industries, homes for scientific workers and their families, and research universities coalesced in distinct clusters around the new emerging suburbs of the 1950s.[13] This agglomeration was supported by the Cold War linking of defense spending and high-tech suburbanization. These Cities of Knowledge were not haphazard creations but the result of deliberate actions by government, defense contractors, and Cold War politics.

The threat of nuclear attack and the targeting of urban centers led to a policy of decentralization underwritten by tax incentives and a civil defense policy that had an immediacy to it. These new Cities of Knowledge should be modest in size and not close to each other.[14] Sprawl had become the national security policy.

Urban decentralization was an old panacea to the problems of decay and congestion that long bedeviled the city. These inherent dangers were extended to embrace Cold War fifth columnists who would find the urban environment hospitable to their subversive agenda. Thus any technology company working on national defense projects critical to the security of the country in this very dangerous nuclear age would be encouraged to move out of the target zone.

But dispersion also appealed to many planners and urban residents who found the post-war cities home to racial conflict, failing public services, deteriorating infrastructure, inadequate transportation, poor schools, and crime, creating an environment of increasing physical danger. Many commentators predicted the end of the city, and the term "white flight" summarized the racial dimension and the pace of the exodus. The suburb seemed to be the antidote to this persistent if not intractable urban crisis. Many who would subsequently seek employment at IBM Kingston were young professionals

mission may not have realized that the promise of prosperity came not because of its own municipal action, but rather from the new centralized state highway authority that had imposed its planning vision on the Hudson Valley and tied the economic health of the region to forces far beyond local control. Indeed this moment represents a loss of agency not only for Kingston, but for many other New York State cities who rejoiced in their connection to the highway to the future. Who could blame them?

In addition to the growing influence of the New York State Thruway Authority, Kingston would find it impossible to escape the Cold War and its reshaping of geography in the atomic age. One of the newest phenomena to emerge from this era was the City of Knowledge, hoping to leave the city for the open, green spaces and natural world of the country.

In the process of migration, we always find push-and-pull forces–factors compelling people to leave a place, such as nuclear danger and urban decay, and the factors drawing the migrants to a new and better place. In the 1950s that place was the suburb—a newly minted and affordable utopia that welcomed the automobile, provided a family home, and threw in a chunk of nature in a federally financed bargain. This scaled-down postwar model of the American dream captured the national imagination and transformed the countryside. It became the locus of this new age.

We can identify with this phenomenon and its appeal to individuals and families. But this suburban migration had a second, long-neglected dimension that involved the American corporation. This new landscape of corporate work, which has been called "pasto-

ral capitalism" by landscape historian Louise Mozingo, responded to the imperatives of managerial capitalism and the changing nature of the research laboratory.[15] The urban landscape could not satisfy these new demands for more space and flexible office arrangements. Corporate managers looked outside the central business districts, now freighted with nuclear vulnerability, to the bucolic fringes. They searched for large tracts of property that would ensure their privacy, promote visibility, and welcome the sprawling, low-rise, horizontal structures—the skyscraper turned on its side—with proximity to major highways. They also required sufficient parking and a landscaped environment that mimicked the university campus from which they would recruit their researchers and engineers. These new suburban campuses would also lure workers from cities to the new pastoral environments where, as *Fortune* magazine noted in 1952, "everyone can work better and think better in the country."[16]

Pastoral Capitalism. Aerial photograph of the IBM Kingston plant, 1966. Collection of Friends of Historic Kingston.

In substituting country work places for the city skyline, business embraced the vocabulary and values of the suburb and identified with the new order. They recognized the redemptive values of the small town with its civility and its bucolic setting that was so closely identified with the traditional American culture.[17] Mozingo argues that the rise of the office park was the "aspirational landscape of a triumphant American capitalism."[18]

The nuclear threat and the urban crisis pushed corporations to search for new homes, and this was now intensified by the changing nature of research and managerial capitalism that required a new kind of laboratory, office, and factory. An emerging consensus pointed to country locations as the right setting for productive and contented workers.

IBM, like many of the major American corporations of the post-war era, supported this suburban ideology and began to look north to the open spaces of Westchester, Dutchess and Ulster counties.[19] By 1953 fifty major New York companies owned property in Westchester. IBM established a foothold in Mount Vernon in 1948 and quickly expanded to Ossining, Cortlandt, White Plains, and Yorktown.[20] IBM had already opened an independent munitions subsidiary in Poughkeepsie in Dutchess County in 1941, and within two years it was absorbed into the IBM corporation. This expansion of the Poughkeepsie plant anchored IBM in Dutchess County and brought the Mid-Hudson into their planning vision.

There is much speculation about the selection of Kingston as an IBM site. Local stories abound about Kingston personalities who influenced Watson Sr. and company officials in the selection the city. In a May 1954 visit to Kingston, Watson met with Fredrick J. Eisler, manager of the Stuyvesant Hotel and a personal friend who, according to the *Daily Freeman*, recommended Kingston for the new factory.[21] Such ruminations neglect the logic of the Kingston choice given the economic and political context of the Cold War for the company and the region. The decentralizing post-war strategy driven by nuclear danger and urban collapse made Kingston, ninety miles north of ground zero, a safe and competition-free zone for development. While those historic forces highlighted the area adjacent to the New York Thruway and its two-hour drive to New York City, the Kingston exit in particular helped pinpoint the city as a desirable location. Thus this selection has an inner logic—a kind of Cold War template.

But, true to the corporate and housing dispositions of the day, the plant would not be within the political boundaries of the city; it would be in the Town of Ulster. While topographical factors were part of the criteria, the movement to the fringe echoed the flight from the urban centers, big and small, and the quest for open undeveloped land. No doubt corporations were eager to avoid what one critic called the "stranglehold" of the city and were not eager to tether their futures to other urban communities even of a more modest scale. In so doing they accelerated the process of post-war suburbanization—indeed IBM's arrival in Ulster provided the underpinning for the county's suburbanization and the transformation of the city of Kingston.

On April 12, 1954, IBM announced plans for a 200-acre plant located in Ulster County one mile outside the Kingston city line. A two-story engineering and administration building, measuring 1,000 feet by 250 feet with a steel frame, would be connected to the manufacturing building with a cafeteria wing. This new plant was to be patterned after other IBM factory buildings. Temporary space for manufacturing was leased in the former Ruzzo Bowlatorium on Grand Street in Kingston.

The factory would consist of low-rise structures, landscaped grounds, on-site parking, security entrances, and improved highway and street access. The construction of IBM Kingston was shadowed by plans for the Kingston Arterial, which would smooth the flow of traffic exiting the Thruway and navigating the streets in and around the city. New York State was determined to remove the Washington Avenue viaduct and restore the road to grade.

By year's end realtors were reporting an uptick in housing starts, especially in the townships of Hurley, west of Kingston, and Ulster, north of Kingston. The growth was attributed to the influx of new IBM home buyers. Indeed city and town officials were excitedly anticipating higher assessments and increased tax revenues. Farm lots, in some instances whole farms, were being bought up quickly. The word "boom" was increasingly being used to describe the IBM impact. There were few warnings. Were communities ready? Did they have the planning mechanisms in place for this speedy transformation?[22]

Kingston, in spite of its public optimism, recognized the complexity and scope of both the opportunities and challenges it faced. The rate and scale of the changes would have caught any municipality unprepared. Kingston, as far as we know, did not recruit IBM as part of a development plan. IBM was the agent of change and thrust itself on the city, but remained outside Kingston's political jurisdiction. The city quickly realized the transformational urgency of the moment and hired Raymond and May Associates, planning and urban housing consultants, to prepare a Comprehensive Development Plan, which was completed in 1961.[23] This document, published only five years after IBM's arrival and no doubt inspired by the new set of conditions, provides a timely assessment of the state of Kingston in the late fifties. The study, commissioned by the Common Council in 1958, contained four sections—an Introduction, Planning Analysis, Comprehensive Development Plan, and Effectuation of the Plan.

The study opens with early admonition to the Common Council to engage in the planning process on a regular basis and in a more public manner. They warned that "reliance on obsolete data has been a serious fault of municipal planning in the past."[24] The deficiency here was magnified by the absence of any planning mechanism in Ulster County. This reaffirms the somnolent quality of city planning—not a particular fault of Kingston, but endemic to small cities. This opening statement suggested a lack of preparation for the onslaught of modernization.

The consultants proposed nine areas for future study, and four of those recommendations were concerned with traffic. Kingston was not yet ready for the automobile frenzy of the post-war period—the catalyst for suburbanization. The urgent need to reimagine highways, roads, and streets as conduits for modernization carrying new residents, new businesses, and even new ideas to an insulated community is an indication of where Kingston stood in the mid-fifties.

The consultants complained that the average citizen was neither adequately informed nor fully engaged in the discussion of civic proposals, and neither was the municipal government alert to state and federal funding sources for new projects.

They reviewed the available vacant land and potential locations for new construction and found over two square miles in parcels exceeding one acre. But these sites were of limited utility because of "topographic features such as steep rocky land in the southwest and eastern portions of the city."[25] They did point to several developable large tracts dispersed throughout the city.

Second Section

The Kingston Daily Freeman

GENERAL NEWS
SPORTS
CLASSIFIED ADS

CITY OF KINGSTON, N. Y., SATURDAY EVENING, DECEMBER 31, 1955.

NINE

1955 Was Greatest Year of Progress in History of Kingston

COUNTY FLOODS CAUSE 10 MILLION DAMAGE

Typewriter Division of IBM Moves to New Kingston Plant

Thruway Completed To Nyack

GOP Achieved Sweep; Cashin Federal Judge

NEW YORK THRUWAY was finally completed with the opening on Dec. 15 of the $60,000,000 bridge spanning the Hudson river between Nyack and Tarrytown.

The section from Kingston to Harriman was opened in November of 1954 and another section from Harriman to Monroe in the spring of this year.

Over 427 mile super-highway, started during the administration of Gov. Thomas E. Dewey. Cost as expected to reach $750,000,000.

REPUBLICANS swept all the principal offices in the city and county elections.

Mayor Fred H. Stang was re-elected by a 2,394 plurality over his Democratic opponent, ex-Mayor William F. Eddelmuth. Former Alderman-at-Large John J. Schwenk returned to politics to defeat Harry A. Flowers Jr. (Dem.) by 2,300 votes.

Republicans retained control of the Common Council, 7 to 6, on the strength of 32 Liberal party votes cast for George Norton Jr. in the sixth ward.

The Democrats picked up eight supervisor seats in the city but the Republicans piled up a substantial 21-17 edge in the county.

Other major GOP candidates elected were: County judge, Louis G. Bruhn; district attorney, reelected, Howard C. St. John; county treasurer, Albert S. Cook.

JUDICIAL honors were heaped on the City of Kingston when President Eisenhower on Aug. 17 announced the appointment of County Judge John M. Cashin to a federal judgeship in the U. S. District Court, Southern District of New York.

President Eisenhower made the interim appointment, subject to approval by the U. S. Senate, at his summer camp at Fraser, Colo.

Judge Cashin, judge of Children's Court since 1943, will have offices at the U.S. Court House, Foley Square, New York city. The Southern District includes the Bronx, New York and the counties of Columbia, Dutchess, Greene, Orange, Putnam, Rockland, Sullivan, Ulster and Westchester.

THE STATE HEALTH Department released figures covering a 10-year study in Kingston and Newburgh on the effects of fluoridation of drinking water on tooth decay in children, a long time controversial subject in health and scientific circles.

Newburgh began adding sodium fluoride to its public water 10 years ago. Kingston did not. The test, according to State Health Commissioner Dr. Herman E. Hilleboe showed this:

Children in Newburgh aged 6 to 9 have 58 per cent less decay, while children aged 13 to 14 show 48 per cent. Six-to-nine-year-olds in Newburgh, whose first permanent molars were erupting when fluoridation began have 41 per cent less tooth decay than Kingston counterparts.

IN EDUCATION, Superintendent Arthur J. Laidlaw retired after 16 years and was succeeded by Earl F. Soper of Norwich, N. Y.

C. Clifford Miller was named principal of Kingston High School, succeeding Theron L. Culver, who resigned on July 1. Stephen G. Hyatt was appointed principal of the Myron J. Michael School and William Reardon principal of Schools No. 6 and No. 8 in the new "double up" policy of the Board of Education.

Union Free School District No. 8 in the Town of Ulster purchased a parcel of the Chambers property to build a 16 class-room school to cost nearly $600,000. Robert F. Herzog was reelected president of the Board of Education.

St. Ursula's dedicated a new $300,000 academy.

FIRE CHIEF Joseph L. Murphy retired after 53 years of fireman's service, including more than 30 as fire chief, and was succeeded by Deputy Fire Chief James M. Brest.

The Hudson Valley volunteers held their annual parade and convention in Kingston — more than 8,000 strong—in a tribute to Chief Murphy, a distinguished service.

FOR RECREATIONAL purposes, the citizens of Kingston found greater pleasure in the new Kingston Point beach which attracted a daily average attendance of 2,063. The zoo at Forsyth Park was refurbished by many new animals and birds imported for the popular rendezvous of children and grownups.

THREE COUNTY hospitals were among the beneficiaries of the $500,000,000 fund showered by the Ford Foundation on the nation's privately supported colleges, universities and hospitals, in history's greatest showing.

Gifts totaling $148,100 were designated as follows:
Kingston Hospital, $60,100.
Benedictine Hospital, Kingston, $62,600.
Veterans Memorial Hospital, Ellenville, $25,400.

KINGSTON'S industrial hopes for the future received another tremendous boost on Nov. 29 when Mayor Fred Stang announced that the Stadelee Realty Corp. of Kingston would construct a $310,000,000 cement plant in the Steep Rocks section.

The downstaters flatly predict the coldest winter and more snow than in the past ten years.

But, on the whole, said Mr. Shultis, it figured to be the severe winter when snow shovels would not see too much use.

George W. Kaufman of Saugerties, former county surrogate, died at the age of 66. Other deaths included: Frederick Dayton Vail, 61, native of Kingston, treasurer of the Motion Picture Association of America, died at Montclair, N. J.; Fred Esslee, 74, proprietor of Hotel Stuyvesant; the Rev. George B. Fagan, 57, former assistant pastor at St. Mary's Church, New York city; Rear Admiral William John Clark Agnew, 63, native of Falls, at San Diego.

IBM TAKES over two North Front street locations. East Kingston home burns to ground while family is away. Hercules Powder Co. paid $100,000 in bonuses to 800 employees. Blasting at proposed cement plant was main concern of persons who attended public hearing. City was to gain by state housing recount. Area Chamber of Commerce favored city-wide toll *(Continued on Page 10, Col. 1)*

DETERIORATION of the downtown section of the city was the topic of considerable and animated discussion among the citizenry, especially those who are affected by the metamorphosis in the downtown area.

Promise of a "new look and better day for the area emerged from a public hearing at the Community Center, where nearly 100 proponents heard plans of progress and rehabilitation.

Rehabilitation of the section in and near the sixth ward area cleared in conjunction with the local housing project, as well as elsewhere in the city housing possible, it was said, through combined efforts of state and federal aid, private capital or a combination of all.

Sections of the fifth and seventh wards are due for consideration, as well as a section of sub-standard dwellings in the sixth ward which are expected to get the most immediate attention.

Spirit runs high among the citizens of downtown who don't want to be by-passed by the city's parade of progress.

DEATH CLAIMED its usual

Summer Produced Fifty 90 Degree Days

RONDOUT ON THE RAMPAGE—During October Floods

Weather Oracles Don't Agree

Thomas P. Shultis, the Freeman's amazingly accurate weather forecaster, and weather bureau oracles at Bear Mountain and New York city disagree slightly in their long-range forecasts for the 1955-56 winter.

Shultis is more optimistic. On Oct. 4 he predicted a warm, dry fall and said the winter weather would be mostly fair, with rainfall below normal. He forecast some cold weather in January, the most severe in February and March.

1955's Hottest

25 Days in Row Of 90 or Better; Record Was 105

Weather Described Hottest in 85 Years

1955 was a year when the weather man gave folks plenty to talk about and most of the talk was uncomplimentary.

It was a year that produced the two biggest floods in 65 years in Ulster county, with property damage of almost 11 million dollars.

It produced the hottest and driest summer in 85 years in the area and throughout New York state.

It was a year that featured, if that's the word, more than 50 days of temperatures in the 90s or above.

And just to be ornery it also produced some of the freakiest weather in local annals.

After a blistering dry spell in which rainfall was several inches below normal all hell broke loose on Aug. 18 and within 48 hours a total of 9.87 inches of rain had pelted the area and caused widespread damage.

The county had hardly dug itself out of the August damage and debris when the rain gods did a more devastating encore on Oct. 14-15-16 as 11.81 inches of rain drenched the county, creating havoc, misery and death.

THE AUG. 18 shower virtually isolated Ellenville and Rosendale, caused two deaths and property damage running into the millions.

Public flood damage for the Aug. 18-19 weekend was set at $1,192,137.50 by Maj. H. Edgar Timmerman, deputy director of Civil Defense in Ulster county. The Board of Supervisors estimated damages to county highways on Page 15, Col. 5)

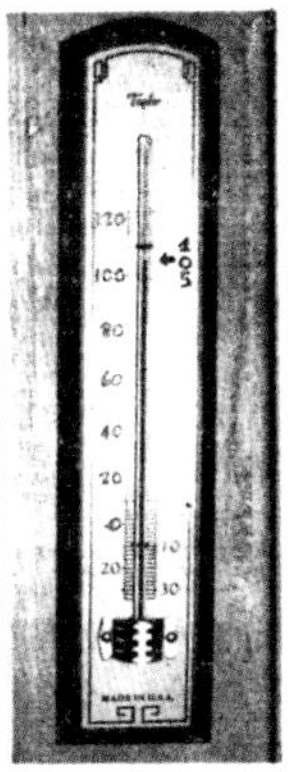

This is how the official thermometer looked on Aug. 5, 1955. It was a sizzling 105 for the year's high. It was even warmer in other parts of the county.

1955 SIZZLERS

May 24	92
July 4	103
July 24	103
August 1	103
August 5	105

CAMERA SWEEP OF IBM—As it looked on Dec. 15, 1955

Expansion Continues In Area

Double Present Force Expected During 1956

(Editor's Note): Material for this article was taken from the Kingston IBM News. Richard O. Gruver is editor, Bertram Burns, news editor, and Edward Casazza, photographer.

International Business Machines Corporation, one of the giants of American industry, quietly rolled up its collective sleeves and went to work in Kingston on Feb. 8, 1955.

Nearly 1,000 employes (942 to be exact) reported for work that day, signalizing the start of a new era in Kingston industry, business and finance.

Since then the number of workers had steadily mounted until it nears the 3,000 mark as 1955 comes to a close. Unofficial estimates of the total eventually to be employed by the regular plant and the typewriter division run twice as high as the 1955 figure.

THE BIG, SPRAWLING plant that lies off the Neighborhood Road north of the city limits typifies the Kingston of the future.

The IBM dream for Kingston developed into substance on Nov. 7, 1953, when Thomas J. Watson, chairman of the board, of IBM, announced plans to construct a major plant in Kingston. The occasion was an IBM Trophy Award Banquet at the IBM Country Club, Poughkeepsie.

In chronological sequence, these are other significant dates in the development of Kingston IBM:

FEB. 1954—Final title to 200 acres of land in the Town of Ulster secured by IBM.

MARCH 19, 1954—Announcement made that the Electric Typewriter Plant would be constructed on newly-purchased site.

APRIL 13, 1954 — Announcement made that contract for construction of IBM Kingston had been awarded to Turner-Campbell, Inc.

MAY 13, 1954—Ground broken for construction.

FEBRUARY 8, 1955 — First Kingston IBMers occupied plant.

FEB. 19, 1955—Project High plant area increase announced, from 320,000 sq. ft. to 459,000 sq. ft.

APRIL 25, 1955—Construction of Electric Typewriter Plant began.

MAY 17, 1955 — Assembly, packing, and shipping of first electric typewriter ever produced at IBM Kingston, product of "pilot line assembly.

SEPT. 22, 1955 — Announcement made that IBM had purchased 300 acres east of the plant for recreational facilities for employes and their families.

SEPT. 28, 1955 — Electric Typewriter Division formed on autonomous basis.

OCT. 20, 1955—Kingston made center of operations for IBM Military Products Division.

THE IBM NEWS of Kingston, in its first issue Nov. 25, 1955 said "enough concrete to lay a three foot wide sidewalk from Kingston to Albany ... enough bricks to build 100 average-size homes ... enough electrical wiring to service the City of Kingston and the Village of Saugerties ... enough blacktop to cover 24 football fields ... were the ingredients of IBM, Kingston.

Literally tons of mortar, steel, *(Continued on Page 15, Col. 7)*

PROGRESS AT BRIDGE—Kingston-Rhinecliff Span, Dec. 15

Area Expansion Needs Planning

Names in News During 1955

Mrs. Edith Zacchoo recovered wedding ring lost 37 years ago at Cuneo's Hotel.

Freeman ad for brewery drivers answered by 100 applicants.

Robert F. Murphy appointed police lieutenant.

Dr. Charles D. Carter retired after 50 years as dentist.

James E. Connelly retired after 49 years employment with The Daily Freeman.

Lt. James P. Martin retired after 37 years on police force.

Kingston Trust Co. observed 35th anniversary with deposits totaling $8,606,546.

Ernest Heppner appointed to State Bridge Authority.

Joe Kelly appointed city editor of Freeman. Irwin J. Thomas assistant city editor.

Area banks reported deposits of $126,000,000.

Newscaster Bob Browning was named the VFW's "Man of the Year.

General Secretary Louis H. Schafer cited for 31 years in YMCA work.

Edwin M. Townsend, 90, still active as custodian of Port Ewen Library.

British frigate docked at Kingston Point.

Lester Langan, 14 Post street baby, survived two-story fall.

Capt. George S. Robinson, USN, cited by French government for services in NATO.

Mrs. Sarah Dean died at 101.

Alfred Mann, 45, Brooklyn, was first county auto fatality in Thruway.

Philetus Johnson of Kingston sent 33 dry fly originals to President Eisenhower.

N. Levan Haver named Fellow of the American College of Trial Lawyers.

Dr. Maurice Silk elected to Fellowship in International College of Surgeons.

Kurdt Cites Need For Cooperation

(Editor's Note: Following is a survey and appraisal of the Kingston area by Albert Kurdt, manager of the Kingston Area Chamber of Commerce, prepared for December 1955 for this special year-end edition of The Kingston Daily Freeman.)

The year of 1955 started on an optimistic note.

As the year progressed it became more and more evident that the expansion and growth of Ulster county was gaining momentum.

The year of 1954 was labeled a "turning point" in the history of Kingston and the entire area. The year 1955 can be called "a year of progress."

The progress and business activity exceeded all expectations.

Unfortunately, there has been a tendency to overlook the closing of a few factories and the reduction in the number of jobs in some others during 1955. Fortunately, the losses have been more than offset by employment gains. A year of rapid expansion accurately describes 1955.

THE MAJOR REASONS for continued expansion are as follows: (1) The employment of over 1,000 men as the result of two major projects alone, the IBM plant and the Kingston-Rhinecliff Bridge; (2) Permanent jobs for over 3,500 persons in four relatively new plants, Rotron Manufacturing Company at Woodstock, Ferroxcube Corporation at Saugerties, Channel Master at Ellenville and IBM near Kingston; (3) The construction of well over 500 homes; (4) Major construction and remodeling of business and commercial properties throughout the area; (5) Construction of new schools, churches, hospitals, highways, streets, etc., and (6) Continued high employment in most of our established industries. Before the end of 1956 we are likely to have 2,000 (*Continued on Page 15, Col. 6)*

Kingston-Rhinecliff That's Official Name

All speculation about the official name of the new bridge across the river above Kingston was ended when the Bridge Authority placed name tablets at both banks of the Hudson. The legend read: "Kingston - Rhinecliff Bridge."

"Greatest Year of Progress." Kingston Daily Freeman, December 31, 1955. Courtesy of Daily Freeman.

IBM and the Modernization of Kingston, New York

41

These conclusions would, however, drive the newcomer to look outside the city and insure that the new housing and corporate development would find the surrounding open rural landscape more inviting.

The demographic studies documented a very slow, negligible rate of growth. This was a city in stasis. From the halcyon days of the late nineteenth century when the population had a growth rate of 11–16 percent, the growth rate had plummeted to an anemic 1.5 percent in 1960. Fifty years of small, barely visible increases insured a low density of 3,954 per square mile, significantly less that Newburgh and Poughkeepsie, suggesting Kingston's rate of development had been slower than its closest urban neighbors.[26] These numbers suggest a community stuck in time and place.

The towns of Ulster and Hurley both doubled in population since the end of the war and, when coupled with areas of open land throughout Ulster County, the suburban pattern of development seemed inevitable. The continuous out-migration from Kingston, which served to underscore this downward pattern, persisted and, according to the consultants, needed to be reversed by "making Kingston a more desirable place to live."[27] This suggestion came in the face of dropping annual birth rates and substantial losses in the 20-to-34-year-old cohort, the latter phenomena a result of "more desirable

TABLE VI-1

POPULATION TRENDS

City of Kingston, Ulster County, and Selected Areas

	CITY OF KINGSTON			Ulster County			Town of Ulster		
		Change			Change			Change	
Year	Population	Number	%	Population	Number	%	Population	Number	%
1870	6,315	--	--	N.A.	--	--	N.A.	--	--
1880	18,344	12,029	190.5	N.A.	--	--	N.A.	--	--
1890	21,261	2,917	15.9	N.A.	--	--	N.A.	--	--
1900	24,535	3,274	15.4	N.A.	--	--	N.A.	--	--
1910	25,908	1,373	5.6	91,769	--	--	N.A.	--	--
1920	26,688	780	3.0	74,979	16,790	-18.3	2,622	-932	-26.2
1930	28,088	1,400	5.2	80,155	5,176	8.6	3,597	975	37.1
1940	28,589	501	1.8	87,017	6,862	6.4	3,993	396	11.0
1950	28,817	228	0.8	92,621	5,604	7.9	4,411	418	10.5
(1957)*	(30,464)	(1,647)	(5.7)	(100,537)	(7,916)	(8.5)	(7,189)	(2,778)	(63.1)
1960	29,260	443	1.5	113,804	26,183	28.3	8,448	4,037	91.5

	Town of Esopus			City of Poughkeepsie			City of Newburgh		
		Change			Change			Change	
Year	Population	Number	%	Population	Number	%	Population	Number	%
1870	N.A.	--	--	20,080	5,354	36.4	17,014	4,436	35.3
1880	N.A.	--	--	20,207	127	0.6	18,049	1,035	6.1
1890	N.A.	--	--	22,606	1,999	9.9	23,087	5,038	27.9
1900	N.A.	--	--	24,029	1,823	8.2	29,943	1,856	8.0
1910	N.A.	--	--	27,936	3,907	16.3	27,805	2,862	11.5
1920	N.A.	--	--	35,000	7,064	25.3	30,366	2,561	9.2
1930	4,167	--	--	40,288	5,288	15.1	31,275	909	3.0
1940	4,220	53	1.3	40,478	190	0.5	31,883	608	1.9
1950	4,738	518	12.3	41,023	545	1.3	31,956	73	0.2
(1957)*	(6,112)	(1,374)	(29.0)	(N.A.)	--	--	(N.A.)	--	--
1960	6,597	1,859	39.2	38,330	-2,693	-6.6	30,979	-977	-3.1

*1957 figures, in parentheses, are not included in the computation of 1960 population changes, and are merely shown as an additional reference.

N.A. = Not Available.

Sources: U.S. Census of Population, Town Development Plan, Town of Ulster.

Population Trends. Kingston Comprehensive Development Plan, Raymond and May and Associates, 1961. Courtesy of City of Kingston Planning Department.

job opportunities and living environments in other areas."[28] Family ties served as demographic anchors keeping the older populations in place and in turn making Kingston an aging community.

The housing stock in Kingston seemed to follow the same trajectory. In 1950, 74 percent of all houses had been built before 1920 and 90 percent before 1930. There had been little new construction in the past fifteen years in contrast to the substantial increase in housing starts elsewhere in Ulster County. This was not only a result of the IBM migration and their suburban housing decisions, but a reflection of Kingston's housing crisis. The selection of the new suburbs made Kingston, with its older limited housing stock, a distant second choice for most IBMers. This is not to discount the significance of the selection of city homes by a modest number of the newcomers who constitute an important component of the story.

The largest number of jobs in Kingston in the late fifties was in manufacturing, specifically apparel and other fabricated textile work dominated by women. The second-largest category included blue collar jobs in the Hudson Cement Company, the Hutton Brick Company, and the Terry Brick Company. Collectively these jobs and the related industries represented a declining and unpromising sector in Kingston's local economy. The hinterland was now threatening to rob

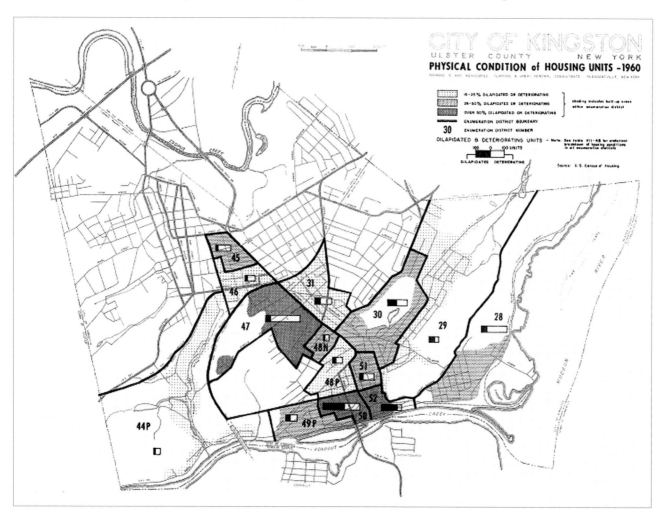

Physical Condition of Housing. Kingston Comprehensive Development Plan, Raymond and May and Associates, 1961. Courtesy of City of Kingston Planning Department.

TABLE VI-3

POPULATION BY AGE GROUPS 1930-1960

City of Kingston, New York

Age Groups	1930 Number	%	1940 Number	%	1950 Number	%	1960 Number	%	Change 1930-40 Number	%	Change 1940-50 Number	%	Change 1950-60 Number	%
Under 5	2,032	7.2	1,810	6.3	2,451	8.5	2,735	9.3	-222	-10.9	641	35.4	284	11.6
5-14	4,311	15.4	4,126	14.4	3,793	13.2	4,770	16.3	-185	-4.3	-974	-23.6	977	25.8
15-19	2,242	8.0	2,278	8.0	1,756	6.1	1,794	6.1	36	1.6	-522	-22.9	38	2.2
20-24	2,292	8.2	2,139	7.5	1,921	6.7	1,536	5.2	-153	-6.7	-218	-10.2	-385	-20.0
25-34	4,162	14.8	4,403	15.4	3,984	13.8	3,344	11.4	241	5.8	-419	-10.1	-640	-16.1
35-44	4,176	14.9	4,125	14.4	4,201	14.5	3,608	12.3	-51	-1.2	76	1.8	-513	-12.2
45-54	3,584	12.8	3,897	13.6	3,851	13.4	3,798	13.0	313	8.7	-46	-1.2	-53	-1.4
55-64	2,793	9.9	2,849	10.0	3,338	11.6	3,276	11.2	56	2.0	489	17.1	-62	-1.9
65+	2,475	8.8	2,962	10.4	3,522	12.2	4,399	15.0	487	19.7	560	18.9	877	24.9
	28,067	100.0	28,589	100.0	28,817	100.0	29,260	100.0						
Unknown	21													
	28,088													

Source: U.S. Census of Population

TABLE VI-4

RACIAL AND ETHNIC COMPOSITION OF POPULATION

City of Kingston, New York

	1930 Number	%	1940 Number	%	1950 Number	%	1960 Number	%
White	27,443	97.7	27,730	97.0	27,958	97.0	27,973	95.6
Non-White	645	2.3	859	3.0	859	3.0	1,287	4.4
	28,088	100.0	28,589	100.0	28,817	100.0	29,260	100.0

Source: U.S. Census of Population.

Population by Age Group. Kingston Comprehensive Development Plan, Raymond and May and Associates, 1961. Courtesy of City of Kingston Planning Department.

the city, with its lack of industrial sites, of jobs as well as potential, but now suburb-bound, residents.

IBM's presence in that first five years had already tipped the scales in favor of the suburbs, with retail sales and wholesale activity in the process of moving out of the city. The consultants noted the rise of shopping centers drawing business away from Kingston. This growing imbalance and the out-migration extended to many businesses from gas stations to restaurants and a host of others.

The first prediction of the consultants based on the previous three decades of Kingston demographic history pointed to extensive population growth in suburbs, and not Kingston. They believed this trend could be reversed, however, if Kingston committed to the development of garden apartments, which would be in a zone of new city growth contributing to a projected population of 40,000 residents by 1980.[29]

This somewhat extended analysis of the state of Kingston makes it abundantly clear that the city needed IBM to stimulate development and foster prosperity—there were no other suitors on the horizon. But a caution is in order, because IBM was not in the city but on its suburban fringe. This is no small matter. What might have been the course of Kingston's history if IBM had chosen to locate its new plant inside the city's boundaries and not on its fringes? However, limited open spaces, the company's suburban predisposition, and the city's immature planning mechanisms all worked against this. While there is little evidence that Kingston courted IBM, and more that it was not a player in the selection process, this may well reflect an intuitive sense on the

The great effect the new IBM plant has had on Ulster County is evidenced by the increase of its industrial index from 42 to 62 between 1954-1958. During this same period the index of both the Mid-Hudson Area and New York State decreased slightly. Data for cities is not yet available.

TABLE VIII-1

EMPLOYMENT BY INDUSTRY GROUP – KINGSTON RESIDENTS

City of Kingston, New York

	1950		1940	
	Number	% of Total	Number	% of Total
Total Population	28,817		28,589	
Employed	12,079	100.0	10,224	100.0
Agriculture, Forestry, and Fishery	98	0.8	105	1.0
Mining	20	0.2	22	0.2
Construction	764	6.3	552	5.3
Manufacturing	3,901	32.3	3,028	29.6
Furniture, Lumber and Wood	179	1.5	84	0.8
Primary metal	26	0.2	44	0.4
Fabricated Metal	19	0.2	6	--
Machinery	263	2.2	134	1.3
Electric Machinery and Equipment	24	0.2		
Motor Vehicles and Equipment	23	0.2	10	0.1
Transportation Equipment	175	1.4	89	0.9
Other Durable Goods	292	2.4	449	4.4
Food and Kindred Products	267	2.2	303	3.0
Textile Mill	327	2.7	195	1.9
Apparel and Other Fabric.Textile	1,694	14.0	1,332	13.0
Printing, Publishing and Allied	133	1.1	106	1.0
Chemicals	350	2.9	238	2.3
Other Non-durable	94	0.8	38	0.4
Not Specified Manufacturing Industry	35	0.3	--	--
Transportation, Communication and Other Public Utilities	1,311	10.9	1,074	10.5
Wholesale Trade	475	3.9	412	4.0
Retail Trade	2,077	17.2	1,829	17.9
Finance, Insurance, Real Estate	325	2.7	266	2.6
Business and Repair Services	322	2.7	206	2.0
Personal Services	788	6.5	975	9.5
Entertainment and Recreation Services	105	0.9	77	0.8
Professional and Related Services	1,214	10.1	1,064	10.5
Public Administration	477	3.9	402	3.9
Not Reported	202	1.7	212	2.1

Source: U.S. Census of Population 1940-1950.

Manufacturing. Kingston Comprehensive Development Plan, Raymond and May and Associates, 1961. Courtesy of City of Kingston Planning Department.

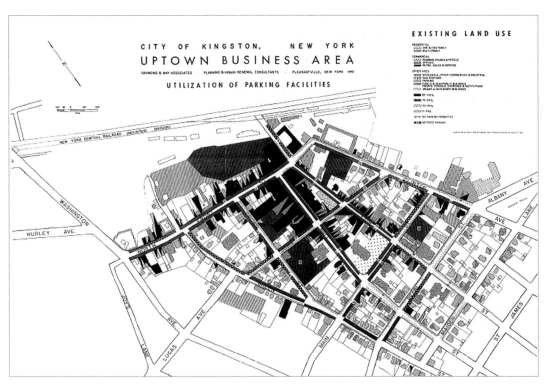

Uptown Business Area Parking. Kingston Comprehensive Development Plan, Raymond and May and Associates, 1961. Courtesy of City of Kingston Planning Department.

city's part that the simple, historic, and slow-paced character of life was threatened with change in unforeseen ways. Indeed the deep suspicion of the company and its workforce, most of whom came from outside the region, suggests not just the reflexive concern about outsiders, but the sense that something more fundamental was at stake and that old Kingston with all its local verities would vanish.

A Mall for Kingston. Kingston Comprehensive Development Plan, Raymond and May and Associates, 1961. Courtesy of City of Kingston Planning Department.

PROPOSED WALL STREET MALL
Uptown Business Area   City of Kingston, Ulster County, New York
RAYMOND & MAY ASSOCIATES · PLANNING & URBAN RENEWAL CONSULTANTS · PLEASANTVILLE, N.Y.

On the other side, the IBM of the mid-fifties was a dynamic international company that was building on its wartime success as a defense contractor providing rifles, bombsights, and engines to the war effort and procuring the Social Security contract. It had prospered and was on the brink of dominating the emerging electronic computing industry. Of course these gains were a testament to the effective political engagement of Thomas Watson Sr. with Franklin Roosevelt and Dwight Eisenhower and his access to the federal government's defense policymakers.[30]

In the fifties the company initiated a program of geographic expansion from San Jose, California, to Lexington, Kentucky, and Kingston, New York. Remarkably, in the period from 1950 to 1960 its workforce would triple and reach 100,000 employees by decade's end. The post-war anxiety about recovery and the Cold War politics made the relationship with the federal government, and especially the Defense Department, critical. These were lessons Thomas J. Watson Jr. took from his father and built on after his accession to the IBM presidency.

One of Watson Jr.'s key strategic moves was to develop the wartime Poughkeepsie site, expand the electric typewriter production, and develop an electronics laboratory.[31] He planted IBM in the Hudson Valley. In addition to a series of technological innovations in electronic computing, Watson Jr. launched an effort to give the company a more streamlined and consistent design format. IBM was morphing into a harbinger of the modern—its products, plants, and furnishings all signaling a deliberate break with ways of the past. What impact would this giant of the new technology have on a city of the past?

IBM slowly but methodically began to rise from the airstrip, and advertisements in the *Daily Freeman* called for assembly line workers who could demonstrate manual dexterity, good eyesight, and mechanical skills. Women handy with tweezers and men with tools should apply, and the call was extended to anyone "who liked serving food or making sandwiches."[32] The early impact of the recruiting effort, which targeted women in the textile industry and clerical work, was to draw off from local businesses the cream of the crop, who were lured by higher wages and the reputation of IBM. While some celebrated this new opportunity, others worried about the collateral pressure to raise wages. Loss of workers and wage inflation fed the growing suspicion of IBM.

Among the early responders to this call was a former Kingston bowling alley employee who pursued a job at IBM with great tenacity. He "called a lot ... and begged for a job." His persistence paid off and he eagerly accepted a job in the cafeteria where he started out washing pots and pans. The narrator was fixated on IBM because of its promise of benefits, retirement, and a secure future—one of the most frequently used descriptors among "beemers" was security. He described IBM as an employer who "recognized those who go the extra mile."[33] His rise was methodical and predictable given his determination and willfulness—indeed it is a remarkable tale that deepens our appreciation for IBM's place in the American narrative. Starting in the

A Kingston Foothold. Ruzzo Bowlatorium, temporary manufacturing floor, 1954. Courtesy of IBM.

kitchen, he rose to become an administrator in personnel and eventually a regional manager as a result, he said, of "taking opportunities." Hard work and promotions yielded two homes; first in the Town of Ulster ($8,000), and then in Hurley ($18,600). He took public speaking classes at IBM to enhance his professional presence and launched a second career in politics. When he retired in 1992, he left a company he "loved and ... felt part of and wanted to be part of."[34]

This first–person account provides an early inside-look into the IBM worker—a character who shares much in common with the archetype of the 1950s, the organization man. William Whyte published the influential *The Organization Man* in 1956, a work that has been mostly caricatured in recent times as a call to arms against the conformity of the 1950s. This publication and other social science tracts explored the changing nature of identify in the post-war corporate world.

Whyte provided a careful and nuanced view of a post-war America increasingly dominated, as he saw it, by the big corporations and the suburban communities they spawned. His work described a critical post-war tension between a new emerging social ethic and the old traditional Protestant ethic with its key principle of rugged individualism. The emerging social ethic proffered a new set of beliefs concentrated around the group as source of creativity and "belongingness," the latter a critical need in the post-war age.[35] Whyte was struggling with the impact of organizational life on individuals who worked in companies like IBM, lived in the adjacent suburbs, and inhabited this self-contained world of work.

The new corporate ethic required workers to identify with the company in exchange for the promise of a lifetime contract and the guarantee of economic stability. This understanding seemed mutually advantageous—loyalty was rewarded with security. However, the underlying fear of Whyte and other social critics was the loss of individualism and its corollary virtue— leadership. The great national anxiety of the fifties was conformity, which many feared was the byproduct of the new corporate ethic.

IBM's introduction to Kingston needs to be understood in the context of the post-war transformation of the United States. Indeed IBM may well represent for Kingston, by virtue of its physical presence, architectural vocabulary, workforce, and technological progress, a simulacrum of the modern age and thus a fundamental challenge to Kingston's traditional world. As suggested above, this difference may have been understood by local residents, many of whom openly articulated a suspicion of the newcomers. The IBM Kingston years represent a fault line in the history of the Hudson Valley. To better understand this key moment we need to look closely at the world IBM created in both the workplace and the community.

The early impact of the recruiting effort that targeted women in the textile industry and in clerical work was to siphon off from local business the most talented, luring them away with higher wages. Those locals hired—and many did get jobs in the first wave of hiring—would receive the best salaries of their young lives.[36]

Applicants submitted to a rigorous one-hour interview that impressed them with IBM's professionalism. One technical writer noted the attraction of IBM's "glamour," which emanated from the excitement of the new computer world and the frontier challenges it offered. In a word, he was "awed."[37] Recruitment extended into local high school classrooms, the labs of General

IBM KINGSTON, N.Y. - VIEW A Looking Northeast- VIEW B Looking Southeast and Close up
of Administration Building . March 23, 1955.

Left: IBM Kingston Plant Construction, 1955. Collection of Friends of Historic Kingston. Below: New Opportunities with IBM. Personnel ad, Kingston Daily Freeman, April 1956. Courtesy of Daily Freeman.

Electric and Bell and other electronics competitors, and even to college campuses, engineering schools, and graduate schools with Ph.D. programs in the sciences. Cooperative education programs at Rensselaer Polytechnic Institute and Northeastern University encouraged undergraduates to spend a semester off-campus in professional work settings with participating companies. These programs provided IBM not only with fresh young minds, but yielded many full-time employees.

While the lure of IBM was powerful, the Hudson Valley countryside also attracted city residents looking for a rural alternative to urban life. The country landscape and the historic character of the region and the city of Kingston were also attractive to the new IBMers; some chose to permanently reside in Kingston itself. They provide an important counterpoint to the sub-urbanization of Ulster County and a caution in generalizing about residential patterns of the new arrivals. Indeed the oral histories provide ample evidence of the powerful effect of Kingston's historical character, which over time recruited many "beemers" to the cause of local history and preservation. They collected published histories, postcards, and artifacts and became active members of the Friends of Historic Kingston. For these residents the past mattered. This challenges the notion of a one-dimensional organization man whose life is defined by the boundaries of the corporate world. Many were able to successfully navigate between these two realms.

One of the essential components of the new social ethic was reflected in the design of the plant's work space, which favored the horizontal over the

Light and the Horizontal. Plugable Unit assembly line, 1955. Collection of Friends of Historic Kingston.

vertical and hierarchical. While critics lamented the loss of individuality and leadership, this design fostered, according to many of the oral histories, a collective approach to work. Teamwork was enshrined as the organizational approach to innovation, planning, and production. This represented a pedagogical commitment to the efficacy of the group and, for Whyte, one of the constituent elements of the organization man. But few of the IBMers interviewed complained of the loss of individuality, and indeed most lauded the collective approach.

Watson Jr. himself was not unaware of the concern for diminished individuality in the work place. He repeatedly emphasized to the public that one of IBM's core beliefs—respect for the individual—was "bone deep." He argued that the organization man is a stereotype and does not apply to all of corporate life. He wrote in 1963:

> IBM has 125,000 employees. A substantial number of them, many of whom I could pick out by name, are highly individualistic men and women. They value their social and intellectual freedom, and I question whether they would surrender it at any price. Admittedly they may like their jobs and the security and salaries that go along with them. I know a few who would put on their hats and slam the door if they felt the organization had intruded so heavily on them that they no longer owned themselves.[38]

The White Shirt. Gary VanVliet, 1972. Photograph by Bruce Whistance.

In almost all of the reported Watson plant sightings, workers noted his charisma, strength and, most critically, his recall of their names, even calling out to them from across a room. This mattered much to both the IBMers and to the Watsons, who we suspect worked hard to cultivate this kind of habit.[39] This pointed counterattack on the organization man thesis is a caution about using that argument to characterize the working habits and private mores of Kingston's IBMers.

However, Watson himself seems to recognize that some loss of individuality has occurred when he complained:

> ... I have some real concerns. It has to do with the cautious attitude of so many young men in middle management today. They seem reluctant to stick their necks out or bet on a hunch. This is not always because they lack will. Sometimes they make mistakes thinking that top management places a greater premium on following form than on anything else. I wish we could stir them up a bit and encourage a little more recklessness among this group of decision makers.[40]

It is safe to conclude, based on Watson's expressed concern, that there was tension between the collective and the individual. Yet many of our narrators felt the bond created by the team was rewarding, productive and, according to one SAGE technician, "exquisite."[41] In several instances the team was seen as compelling loyalty, and the team's standards and expectations deepened the commitment to the task at hand. We can appreciate in this attitude an effort by companies and workers to counter any loss of individualism with an approach that cultivated a sense of collaboration. The satisfaction from this experience endured and has been recalled with warm and positive words. One programmer believed that, "these were great people ... pleased to work with ... talented, competent and bring out the best in you."[42]

We begin to sense here the outlines of an IBM culture that would not only shape the work experience but influence the course of Kingston's history. Loyalty played a powerful role in maintaining this culture—it was the social glue of the company.

Key events in workers' lives were marked by a range of company responses aimed at acknowledgment of the personal—birthday celebrations, team awards dinners, family days, bereavement support, and fondly remembered retirement roasts—all of which, while strengthening bonds with the company, were designed to counter the sense of the impersonal and placelessness produced by IBM's transfer policy. While many understood this policy to be an essential part of their career path and necessary for promotion and advancement, others successfully resisted and lived to tell the tale. IBM's policy aimed to neutralize the dangers of the organization man—Whyte's "transients" who left home and uprooted their lives from families, friends, and professional colleagues. This process of uprooting had been institutionalized by IBM and became one of the defining elements of the post-war economy.

At one level we should not be surprised at a program that embodies the principle of job mobility. Indeed for much of our history Americans have associated movement with economic progress—it is a foundational concept. But what is new here is the scale and internationalization of the process and its identification with one company—"I'm Being Moved." Indeed the uprooting was sweetened by moving subsidies and a promise from Tom Watson Jr. that when a person was relocated he or she was entitled to a substantial increase in responsibility and pay. He complained that too many of these moves were made for the convenience of the company rather than the benefit of the employee.[43]

IBM created men who could fit in anywhere. This training, as one IBM executive noted, "makes our men interchangeable."[44] For Whyte this policy has less to do with individual difference and more to do with the homogenization of place and the creation of a national culture in which moving about becomes easier.[45] So Kingston would be one stop on this corporate journey and, unlike a homegrown indigenous business, would have workers in transit who would impact in special ways on the city and its neighboring communities.

The expectation of the worker's willingness to pick up and go is built on the assumption that the company is the surrogate home base and that the employees will together create instant communities wherever they go. Here is the symbiotic relationship between IBM and Kingston's instant suburbs.

IBM's vaunted reputation for supporting community involvement by its employees and its direct financial contributions to a variety of local organizations is a part of their underwriting of "belongingness." This is not to denigrate the community commitment ideal, but to locate it in the context of the company's philosophy. One individual, a World War II veteran, Kingston resident, and IBM manager, believed the company "wanted you to be involved."[46] He served as a member, and in many cases an officer as well, of the Lions Club, the Hospital Foundation Board, Boy Scouts, Girl Scouts, Big Brother, Big Sister, and even helped organize the IBM-sponsored Big Blues Band. He felt he wanted to "give back" to Kingston.

"Volunteer Bob," an IBM diagnostic engineer, was given a list of community organizations to consider, and he responded by joining the Salvation Army Advisory Board where he stayed for eighteen years. He then became involved in a series of community charity races and sat on the Executive Board of the Boy Scouts. He was honored by the Kingston Kiwanis for his extensive volunteer work.[47]

Employees were given release time for community projects, and members of the emergency ambulance and fire services were called to duty at work using the company's factory-wide communication system. Individuals remember being gently prompted to get involved.

"Beemers Camaraderie." Celebrating St. Patrick's Day. Photograph by Bruce Whistance.

This abiding commitment to community service was not only through individual engagement, but company actions as well. Many institutions received financial support from IBM—the Kingston Hospital was near the top of the list. The roots of the corporate paternalism, a term with a negative connotation suggesting self-interest disguised as beneficence, comes from the need to force-feed belongingness and encourage workers to move out of the factory into the social world around them. However, this sensibility challenges the organization man's singular commitment to the company and the all-encompassing world of work.

Community engagement was part of IBM's public persona, related to its commitment to customer service and, for the Watsons, a corporate mantra. Service to the customer and service to the community were interdependent actions, both working to enhance the company's reputation. Providing the best customer service was one of the three core principles articulated by Thomas J. Watson Jr. in his 1963 "Business and Its Beliefs" manifesto, along with respect for the individual and a commitment to perfection.[48]

Thus the public face of the company displayed to Kingstonians by IBMers would provide more direct contacts and critically influence their first impression. The IBM uniform of white shirt, dark pin-striped suit, rep (preppy) tie, and wing-tip shoes distinguished them from most community residents, whose daily dress was far less

formal. This costume also signaled a seriousness of purpose and respect for the customer, and even extended to computer repairmen who were required to wear the uniform when in the field and carry their tools in a briefcase and not a tool bag.[49] One local real estate broker suggested the formality of the dress communicated to the public not just a polished quality but a "haughtiness."[50] Others commented on the "sense of entitlement" displayed by some IBMers.[51] (One local realtor lamented the loss of the white shirt and tie later in the Kingston years, believing that the result was a diminution of respect and seriousness.)[52] Thus one IBM custom intended to communicate professionalism and respect was interpreted by some as a sign of aloofness and distance. The conflicting interpretations of the dress code are illustrative of the problems of cultural dissonance when a major company moves to a small tradition-bound city.

This sense of aloofness was exacerbated by the secrecy that surrounded the work at IBM Kingston. For a local undertaker, the plant was a "mystery to him." When he asked, "What did the deceased do?" family and relatives responded, "I do not know." He claimed he never did get an answer. Even an IBM wife complained that she "never understood what it was," and the best she got from her husband was that it was "classified material." While some of this was a result of the defense contracts and special projects and the technical nature of the work, much of it came from a separation of work and home—a barrier that was fortified by corporate practice and contributed to the view of IBMers as elitist and exclusive and profoundly distant from the locals.

The internal world of IBM Kingston was a critical element shaping the relationship between the city and the company. The values and mores of the organization shaped its workers, equipping them with the tools for developing a sense of belongingness, and in turn would provide the foundation for the dialogue with Kingston. They would have to bridge the world of traditional, small-town America and the new technological world of the computer age.

"Togetherness." Collection of Susan Levangia.

Kingston did not recruit IBM and understandably was not prepared for the company's massive presence in the community. In this lack of preparation Kingston was not alone in the post-war world, a world where often the pace of change left most municipalities playing catch-up. But catch up it did.

Nothing better illustrates this than the state of Kingston traffic described earlier. The city had operated without stop signs and traffic lights given the modest number of automobiles passing through. Street improvements, new traffic flow patterns and traffic controls were introduced after IBM's arrival. The automobile was invading Kingston. The highway infrastructure, with the help of state money, was improved with better access roads to the city including the removal of the Washington Avenue viaduct, the creation of a direct link to the Thruway, Routes 28, 9W, 209 and, especially, Interstate 587—one of the shortest interstate highways, constructed to meet the needs of IBM.[53]

The opening of the Kingston-Rhinecliff Bridge in February 1957 after a long, thirteen-year wait was hailed by Kingston Mayor Stang "as another decisive step forward in Kingston's march of progress." The river-based communities of Kingston and its Dutchess County neighbors would now share a revivified commercial life and respond to IBM's growing demand for new housing. One member of the New York State Bridge Authority, John S. Stillman, stated it was the aim of the Authority to promote the Hudson Valley and bring more industry to the region. He cited the "importance of IBM just over the hill for its contributions the area's development."[54]

The new transportation network was both a byproduct and catalyst for IBM Kingston. As the size of the workforce increased and the scale of production accelerated, these new roads would move people and goods more efficiently and connect the city to modern roadways that it could never afford to develop with its limited municipal budget. One consequential byproduct of the transportation revolution was to integrate Kingston more fully into the communities of knowledge in the Hudson Valley and New York City. However, though transportation did improve, it was not enough to bridge the emerging urban-suburban divide.

The widespread suspicion that greeted IBM's arrival is a good indication of the cultural gap that separated the city and the company. One former Long Islander who migrated to Kingston in the 1980s did not want to be identified as a New Yorker, which he believed carried a negative connotation. He worked hard to slow down, blend in, and adapt to local ways. He felt his Long Island accent had to be muted to enable him to assimilate in a very rooted community. In spite of this awareness he remained an outsider.[55] One native Kingstonian described the city as a place "frozen in time," sleepy, stratified, and with little upward movement. Businesses were small and family-run operations, she noted, and "you knew who you were from where you lived." Natives described "beemers" as carpetbaggers—not a flattering term. "Who are these people?"[56] "Who do they think they are?" "They are taking over." The growing fear of displacement rose up from a staid community whose citizens may have been anxious about losing their local position as citizens of importance, as well as their familiar pace of life.[57]

One IBMer believed that the resentment was based on some mythical views of the company, especially its work and pay. He felt that he and his colleagues were criticized for not appreciating the area and its history.[58] Many newcomers, in the face of a sleepy night life—"lights went out at 6 p.m."—couldn't wait to get out of town and make the 92-mile drive to New York City. One observer commented on "the sparks out of the back wheels of cars" during the Friday night exodus.

Parking on the Corporate Campus. Photograph 1955, looking northeast. Collection of Friends of Historic Kingston.

Driving and Dining. D-D's Drive-In.

This resentment endured for a generation and resurfaced after the plant's closing in 1994. One former IBMer turned radio station owner and broadcaster felt the company was held to a different standard, and he wondered if "oh my god we should have treated them better."[59] But not all agreed with this wistful statement. The depth of the resentment was echoed in comments like "good riddance" and "now we can get back to normal."[60]

These sentiments not only reveal the cleavage between the two worlds, but they are the context for the decision by newcomers about where to live. The constraints of the housing stock in Kingston—old homes with little new construction—in 1955 drove IBMers out of town and into the undeveloped areas of the Town of Ulster and elsewhere in Ulster County. They made this choice deliberately in an effort to bypass the circumscribed nature of Kingston, as they saw it, and chose instead places to build new communities where their voices would shape local politics, education, and culture. Thus in these new suburbs they would make the critical decisions for the future and shape the geographical landscapes of the region.

Initially, the demand for apartments and rental units in the mid-fifties exposed Kingston's unpreparedness and provoked a long discussion about the state of housing in the city. But the scale of the growing need was extensive, and under the best of circumstances Kingston would have a difficult time meeting the demand. Developers, real estate brokers, and the new arrivals now turned their eyes to the Town of Ulster, just outside of Kingston, and the available farmland ideally suited for tract housing. The population of the Town of Ulster increased from 4,411 persons in 1950 to 8,449 residents in 1960, an increase of 91.5 percent. The housing stock, unlike Kingston's older inventory, was new; only 22 percent was built before 1950. As IBM's population grew, the Town of Ulster added 948 new homes between 1950 and 1959, another 1,108 units between 1960 and 1969, and between 1970 and 1979 an additional 911 new units. By century's end 78 percent of the town's housing stock had been constructed after the arrival of IBM.[61]

Much of this construction was concentrated in Lake Katrine, Lincoln Park (Sunset Park), Hillside Acres, Halycon Park, and Whittier, all communities that were small hamlets surrounded by farms and set in the rural countryside. The last-named, Whittier, was

Rondout before Urban Renewal. Broadway looking east from East Union Street, Rondout, 1969 or earlier. Collection of Friends of Historic Kingston. Note the Urban Renewal Relocation Office sign. The entire left-hand side of the street was demolished in 1969.

described by one "beemer" as an "IBM ghetto." In these communities people and their families socialized with coworkers and endowed the instant suburbs with connection and rootedness. One programmer who initially owned a home in Kingston complained that he "did not feel warmly welcomed, with little neighborhood mixing of people and not close to his nearest neighbor." His remedy was to build a home in Hurley.

Housing developments were not limited to the Town of Ulster, but spread north to Saugerties, west to Hurley and east to Red Hook. This pattern is unlike the traditional pattern of

Lawns Replace Farms.

suburbanization in which a city's population overflows its boundaries and the out-migration of residents to the country is to its newly built suburban communities. In that case the centrifugal process moves outward from a central city, with most of the migrants retaining some connection to the center through work, family, and even culture. The development of the cluster of IBM suburbs is a centripetal process in which new, instant suburbs are loosely tethered to the center and have no historical connection to the city. In the latter approach the relationship needs to be nurtured, and the city center has to work to attract the suburbanites. Thus Kingston's new suburbs are not extensions of the center, but grafts onto the city. IBM's location, just outside the city's boundaries in the Town of Ulster, linked Kingston to its new, outlying suburbs where they shared many of the interdependencies of cities and suburbs, but as an inchoate metropolitan community.

The architectural vocabulary of the post-war suburban home included three basic styles—the Cape, the ranch, and the split level. These styles had been seen in the early fifties on Long Island and, not surprisingly, many of the same developers now set their sights on Ulster. The Cape Cod with its colonial roots, rediscovered in the 1920s, appealed to the post-war buyer because of mass production and low cost. It offered two bedrooms on one floor, and it would be modified for Kingston. As expectations and families grew, the split level became the alternative to the Cape. This home added a second story with additional bedrooms, an integrated garage, and a standard lot size. The last iteration was the ranch house, a sprawling, low-lying, one-floor home with ample windows to open the structure to the outside. The basic design of these three types of homes, though adapted and reformatted by builders and owners, can be seen in great numbers in Kingston's suburban neighborhoods. They reflect the nature of family life and provide social clues to the way of life of "beemers."

The housing boom exerted great pressure on the utility companies to not only meet the demand of new homes, but to provide the energy necessary to support an array of new appliances including water heaters, washers, dryers, ranges, air conditioners, and many other labor-saving devices—a good indication of the standard of living and the quality of life expectations of the IBM newcomers.

The choice of these new suburban communities not only reflected IBMers' desire to live in a place where they would exercise control, but also foreshadowed the inevitable linking of residence and schooling. The influx of highly trained workers, frequently with graduate degrees in the sciences and engineering, put new stresses on the school system. Educated themselves and ambitious for their children, the newcomers would not only increase enrollments, but pressure the system on behalf of their children. The one-room schoolhouse and the intimate classroom environment where you know all your classmates and had been together for years would have a hard time surviving this onslaught.[62]

The urgent need for new elementary schools, requiring budget outlays and tax increases, led to a series of bitter debates, rejected budgets, defeated bond issues, double kindergarten sessions, and community divisions. The issues here and the ensuing divisions are self-explanatory. But this kind of battle would touch raw nerves, pitting the needs of children against concerns about higher school taxes. The debates would spill over to school consolidation, location of new schools, and even curriculum at the high school level. And of course all of the struggles were a result of the influx of uninvited newcomers. The conflicts were magnified and made more public when those new students entered the school system, often shadowed by concerned parents who were nervous and anxious about the quality of the education. In time the system changed and, as the oral histories document, the level of satisfaction improved.

The automobile, which dominated this suburban culture, gave residents a shopping choice. Would they journey into Kingston or shop at one of the new shopping centers? Traffic problems, parking issues, and the traditional nature of many stores in Kingston made it difficult for the city to compete. A proposal in March of

1955 to build a shopping center on Albany Avenue near the IBM plant was a harbinger of things to come. The developers noted that shopping centers, "shopping on wheels," were taking the country by storm. Their proposal would "enable cars to park within 10 to 12 feet of the front of the building. A covering like a visor will project out about ten feet from the front of the center making it possible for patrons to step from their automobiles ... an advantage in case of inclement weather."[63] The local developer pointed to the Yonkers Cross County Shopping Center as a worthy model. In January 1956 a second proposal targeted the same area north of the city with 40 stores and 2,000 parking spaces on 30 acres of land adjacent to the Kingston Arterial. Another shopping center was proposed for the Town of Esopus on Route 9W. Kingston was soon to be surrounded by shopping centers. By the late seventies these centers were morphing into malls, with more stores and a whole range of additional customer services including movies and restaurants. The Hudson Valley Mall opened in 1981 on one level with over 70 stores extending over 700,000 square feet and adjacent to the Hudson Valley Plaza. Increasingly the retail trade was leaving Kingston and relocating north along Albany and Ulster Avenues. Easily accessible from the new IBM suburbs by car, with ample parking and a breadth of products that met the needs of the new consumers, the malls accelerated the marginalization of the commercial center of Kingston.

Above left: Wall Street Struggles. At left: Anchor Stores. Wall Street, Uptown Kingston, mid-1960s. Above right: The Malling of Kingston. Kings Mall with Mayfair Theatre.

Columbia historian Kenneth T. Jackson concluded, "that as malls mushroomed central business districts faltered." For Jackson the mall was "at the core of a worldwide transformation in distribution and consumption."[64] We see this pattern vividly played out in Kingston.

Municipalities—from city to town and hamlet—recognized their lack of preparedness in coping with the IBM type of invasion. Planning consultants were hired and local planning commissions were established. But much of this was playing catch-up. This is not to fault Kingston for their planning deficiencies, for in this matter they were representative of other communities of this size. In 1955 Kingston, as a requirement for Assistance for Urban Renewal, had to prepare a comprehensive master plan, its first. The Town of Ulster's first comprehensive plan did not appear until the sixties. A former Kingstonian and well-regarded urban planner endorsed the notion of metropolitan planning for the city and its suburbs, warning that "you can't think of planning in Town of Ulster without considering the City of Kingston."[65] We see here one of the earliest recognitions of the metropolitan character of IBM's impact. Indeed the economic health of the city center depended on this kind of cooperation. But the recommendations of planners and their plans are at best advisory and do not carry the force of law. Kingston Mayor Stang, addressing the concerns of the moment, said:

> I think that these years will be recorded as having seen the City shake free from a state of lethargy. ... For too long those in charge were like an ostrich. They stuck their heads in the sand and refused to recognize the situation. ... too many people were riding the coattails of others and that was not a healthy condition.[66]

IBM appeared so quickly and on such a large scale, accompanied by a benign reputation, that the city lost agency and had little control over events. But IBM and its staff, infused with good planning instincts and experience, would, through its employee loan program and commitment to community service, help Kingston modernize its planning process. This two-dimensional engagement with Kingston, augmented in many cases by direct financial support such as a $100,000 anonymous gift to the YMCA in the 1980s, worked its way into the city's fundamental operations.[67] One local long-time member of the Lions Club counted over seventy members from IBM.[68]

IBM changed the demographic profile of the area, and a coterie of young people entered the life of Kingston and brought fresh energy to old institutions like the public library, where one programmer became an active member of the Friends of the Library and ran the book sale for years. Kingston's city historian recalled that the Salvation Army Advisory Board and the Friends of Historic Kingston were populated with IBMers.[69] The Ulster Fire Department counted "beemer" volunteers among its crews.[70] IBMers were ubiquitous and became part of Kingston's urban fabric.

The tendency to focus on the business and machine aspect of the company has often neglected the company's international dimension both as an economic and cultural force. The posting to another country is the most obvious example. A three-year assignment in Germany enabled one programmer and his family to learn a second language and live in another culture for an extended period of time. One "beemer" invited his neighbor to visit him during his Paris posting, an action he saw as a modest contribution to the cultural life of Kingston. When IBM hired Egyptian, Palestinian, and Jordanian engineers, they introduced Muslim culture and Middle East politics to Kingston. This was one of the ways that IBM contributed to the cosmopolitanism of Kingston.[71]

Over time the notion of the organization man focused solely on his work came to be challenged by the deep commitment of IBMers to local history. They collected maps and local history books, postcards, photographs and prints, IBM publications, and ephemera.[72] They became local tour guides sharing their knowledge of the city's streets, stone houses, and historic buildings. A few volunteered at the Trolley Museum, while some moved back to the city, purchased old houses, and restored them with great care. Others joined local historical societies in many Ulster County towns and villages. And most significantly they were involved in the founding of the Friends of Historic Kingston in 1965.[73] The Friends worked to establish historic districts and the landmarking of buildings, and created a preservation fund. The ongoing engagement of former IBMers and their sustaining membership suggests an abiding connection to Kingston and its history. The company's commitment to preservation was evident with the $100,000 IBM gift to restore the Broadway Theatre and thereby to "increase the city's cultural and economic appeal."[74]

In this remarkable bridging of their work at the frontiers of modern technology with a care and love for local history, IBMers brought work and vocation together in a unified vision. This is perhaps a paradoxical return to the historic sensibilities we discovered in the tricentennial celebration of 1952.

It is understandable that IBM would influence planning, housing, transportation, and education in Kingston. This is not surprising given the scope and size of the company. However, there is danger that if one focuses only on these major categories the pervasiveness of IBM's reach will be missed. There were few businesses and few households that were not touched by the company's presence.

In January 1995 Alex Bahl, the owner of Rafalowsky's Men's Store, initially on Broadway and later moved to Albany Avenue, announced he was closing the store after eighty-one years in Kingston. Bahl had bought the business in 1983. He blamed the closure on the 1993 layoffs at the IBM plant. IBM had accounted for 50 percent of his customers, whose formal dress code fed his tailoring business for years. Bahl also complained about the national dress-down movement, which had contributed to IBM's relaxation of its white shirt standard and Bahl's declining profits.[75]

A local automobile dealer claimed that IBM's business "made him and almost broke him" in thirty years of dealing with them. He acknowledged that it was good to do business with them because "you never had to worry about the financing." He sold mostly Buicks, which he classified as a "luxury" item, and in 1982 added the upscale Saab to his showroom. The departure of the IBMers cut his business by 30 percent and sent the dealership into a tailspin. He believed IBM "made" his business.[76]

There are many more illustrations of IBM's economic influence in the commerce of Kingston, from funeral directors to energy providers. But these examples need to be placed alongside the impact on community organizations from volunteers and direct financial support.

Religious institutions are important as expressions of faith and religious beliefs, but also play a key role in constructing "belongingness." For newcomers, churches, synagogues, temples, and meetinghouses establish networks of like-minded people who are searching for a congenial environment for integration into their new community. The IBM influx expanded the population of most denominations. One example is Temple Emanuel, which had many IBMers in its congregation.[77] The existing temple on Abeel Street became too small and faced a geographic shift of its membership; moreover, it was eager to expand its educational space. It needed a new location and would eventually be moved

Temple Emanuel, Albany Avenue, Kingston. Photograph 2013 by Stephen Benson.

to better serve the new emerging suburbs north of the city. Chairman Kalish stated that, "a growing and more alert Kingston needs and deserves a larger and more fitting House of God."[78] The concern for the religious instruction of the young congregants was shared by many religious denominations, which recognized the changing demographic of Kingston's metropolitan region.

The Roman Catholic Archdiocese was not far behind. In September 1957 it purchased five acres at the intersection of Route 9W and Boice's Lane. The action was taken "in light of an expansive building program in the town of Ulster brought about by the location of the IBM plant here." The influx of Catholic families had taxed the capacities of the parishes of the city.[79]

In post-war suburbs new arrivals generally showed a strong preference for a church that united denominations and minimized doctrinal differences. What mattered to them was a church that was useful and stressed fellowship.[80] This attitude grows out of the quest for "belongingness" and found a home in the community church movement. On April 8, 1956, a nondenomina-

tional church, the Community Drive-in Church, opened on Route 9W. Its services would be "undenominational" and broad in conception. A local minister explained that "the challenge is upon us to break out of the old categories of thought and the ever new dynamic and inclusive will of God for the masses."[81] Five hundred residents turned out for the service that offered "practical preaching designed to reach new residents of the area."[82]

This represents a small sampling of IBM's impact on Kingston and its suburban neighbors. The breadth and variety of the companies, organizations, institutions, and family businesses drawn into this new economic, social, and culture nexus reinforces the sense of the ubiquity of IBM. The interconnectedness was so long-standing that after a generation it seemed normal.

Beginning in the 1980s, as the PC revolution gained momentum, IBM began to slip from its dominant position in the industry. IBM watched its earnings drop precipitously, and the company began to hemorrhage billions of dollars. A slow and unpublicized reduction of the workforce began after 1985. Then, in March of

1993, the unthinkable occurred. At 11 a.m. on a Monday early in the month, Joe Claudio was summoned to his manager's office in the Kingston plant, an event that in better times had been synonymous with promotion or relocation. But in the current climate, anticipating the worst, he said, "Do what you've got to do."[83] Later, a friend of Claudio's and a father of two boys announced that, "I am all washed up." An era—the era of virtually absolute job security—had ended. At Zenon's, an Ulster Avenue bar near IBM, the mood was angry and hostile. Many complained that this was not the same company— an assertion that was widely held by former IBMers. In the following months informal groups of former employees sprung up throughout the neighborhood to talk about "life after IBM."

The break with the past seemed so radical and the firings so out of character that the only way to make sense out of the events was to separate the past from the present. This bifurcation of the company's history may not have come exclusively out of the course of events, but rather a recognition that the change of practices and policies reflected a deep fundamental break with the past. Critics argued that the Watsons' credo of balancing profits against the well-being of the employees and the nation's interest as a necessary duty for companies helps explain why Watson Sr. avoided layoffs during the Depression. At the top of CEO Louis Gerstner's 1994 list, however, was shareholder value, now "the primary measure of success."[84]

The Rubicon had been crossed and IBMers in Kingston now faced the unthinkable—layoffs. By 1994 the 2.5 million square feet of space and 7,100 employees were reduced to a corner of the plant with only 1,500 workers.

In July of 1994, Louis Gerstner announced, in spite of early public denials, the closing of IBM Kingston, driving the shrinking total IBM workforce to a low of 220,000 by year's end. These actions hit at one of the central principles of the organization—the promise of job security, a practice with a long and durable history at IBM. Indeed this practice was one of the most powerful expressions of its corporate paternalism, one which softened the uprooting of employees and blunted the talk of unionization. Security was an important adhesive in the building of the instant suburbs for the transient newcomers, providing them with an anchor in post-war America. Most importantly it inoculated them against the fear of being unhinged, merely free-floating bodies in an impersonal world of work.

Some were lucky and, either through an intuitive sense that things were not well or from a warning from a concerned colleague, retired in 1991 and 1992, usually with full retirement benefits. Others were transferred to Poughkeepsie or other IBM locations. But many were asked to "turn in your badge."

The growing sense of dislocations began to spread. Almost every aspect of Kingston's life was affected. No one was prepared, neither IBMers nor the city of Kingston.[85] The community appeared frightened, unsure what to do and without any backup plan. Inevitably the exodus of the company and its professional employees began to cut into every aspect of the life of the city. IBM's financial support for the arts, cultural, and a broad range of other community organizations dried up. The pool of volunteers who maintained these groups— some of its most capable and skilled members—moved away. The housing market went into free fall and, as "for sale" signs were posted in front of the second, third, and fourth house in a neighborhood, prices dropped quickly. IBM children who required new schools, improved curriculums, and came with high expectations were leaving. The tax base, essential for maintaining these schools, was shrinking as well. The city and the surrounding towns found it increasingly difficult not only to staff their committees and commissions, but to pay their bills. Automobile dealers and undertakers, restaurants and supermarkets, and even the malls felt the squeeze. One Kingston barber estimated a 25 to 30 percent loss in his customer base, a parameter that was cited by many businessmen.

In assessing the loss of IBM, a successful automobile dealer noted that the company had been very

Main Post Office Demolition, 1970.

generous to the community, indeed "they made the town."[86] Another local businessman felt that, "the dollars had left Kingston … the anchor was pulled out … devastating."[87]

But the dollars were not the only thing that left Kingston. In January 1995 the Hudson Valley Blood Service announced that blood supplies had reached dangerously low levels—Kingston and the region were running out of blood. Officials attributed the shortage to the flu and IBM's exit and explained, "We used to get a tremendous amount of blood from IBM … used to have three or four blood drives a year."[88]

Many residents warned of "the danger of putting all our eggs in one basket." This was an often repeated post-mortem that had as a subtext the notion of retribution. The effort to try to make sense out of a shocking reversal of fortune pointed to the idea that the company town was a fundamentally flawed economic organism.[89] We can find examples of this failure in U.S. Steel in Homestead and General Motors in Flint. The argument is that dominant employers foster dependency in their communities.[90] One needs to recall that Kingston had a passive role in IBM's original decision to locate in their city. And what choice was there at the time to reject their overture in the face of a stagnant local economy and population stasis? How could Kingston have resisted?

We might try to indict IBM for breaking the social contract and acting with cold indifference toward Kingston. But the parties here had no reciprocal understanding; indeed the city fathers in the early years became indiscriminate boosters of the Coming.

One way to evaluate the IBM legacy, apart from the effort to fix responsibility, is to measure and critique the changes in Kingston resulting from the generation-long relationship. IBM contributed a core group of well-educated young citizens to Kingston and the new suburbs they inspired. These newcomers played a crucial role in municipal government, community organizations, education, housing, and preservation, and they raised the standard of living. They were an engaged class cutting across many areas of Hudson Valley life and in the end making Kingston a cosmopolitan city. The professionalism, standards of work, preparation, sense of purpose, breadth of knowledge, and internationalism they brought to their civic engagements helped modernize Kingston.

IBM's arrival generated a host of problems that compelled Kingston to deal with a broad range of issues on an unimagined scale. While many of the responses were improvised and ad hoc, the cumulative impact was to compel Kingston to reinvent itself and ironically enable the city to meet the challenges of the future without IBM. No small matter.

What will endure is the memory of the IBM generation in Kingston, which, in spite of the sense of loss and disappointment, offers a historic reminder of a time when things were good. This essay began by citing the importance of history to Kingston's identity and contemporary life. We have now begun to add the IBM Years to that story and reflect on the meaning of this important period in the city's history. In time the pain and disruption of the recent past will recede and we will come to see this era with new and fresh eyes as a key chapter in Kingston's modernization. ⊙

Roger Panetta is a Visiting Professor of History and Lecturer at Fordham University and is a Visiting Scholar at the Brooklyn Historical Society focusing on waterfront history. He has authored numerous articles on the history of New York State and served as Adjunct Curator for History at the Hudson River Museum. He edited Dutch New York: The Roots of Hudson Valley Culture *in 2009 and* Westchester: The American Suburb *in 2006. He coedited, with Eileen Panetta,* On Shattered Ground: A Civil War Mosaic *(Penguin Books, 2013), coauthored* The Hudson: An Illustrated Guide to the Living River *(Rutgers University Press), and authored* The Tappan Zee and the Forging of the Rockland Suburb *(Historical Society of Rockland County, 2010). He is Curator of the Hudson River Collection at Fordham University, and in 2006 received the Cultural Heritage Award from the Lower Hudson Conference (now Greater Hudson Heritage).*

Notes

1   Andrew S, Hickey, *The Story of Kingston* (New York: Stratford House, 1952), 212–214; "Kingston Festival," *New York Times*, March 30, 1952.

2   Hickey, 212–214; "Kingston Festival," *New York Times*, March 30, 1952.

3   Kirmess is a Dutch country festival or carnival.

4   Alf Evers, *Kingston, City on the Hudson* (Woodstock, New York: The Overlook Press, 2005), 368. Much of this discussion draws on Evers, 352–390.

5   Evers, 370–373.

6   Michael Fine, *Public Works: New York Road Building and the American State*, Ph.D Dissertation, Brandeis University, 2003, pp. 336–343.

7   Fine, 395–397.

8   Fine, 397.

9   "400 Attend Rites Held at Change," *Daily Freeman*, October 26, 1954.

10 "Quarter of U.S. Population Lies Close to Kingston Area," *Daily Freeman*, February 24, 1954.

11 "Hudson Cities See Boom in Thruway," *New York Times*, February 23, 1954, v.

12 Ibid.

13 Margaret Pugh O' Mara, *Cities of Knowledge: Cold War Experience and the Search for the Next Silicon Valley* (Princeton and Oxford: Princeton University Press, 2005), 1–2.

14 O'Mara, 2–3.

15 Louise A. Mozingo, *Pastoral Capitalism: A Survey of Suburban Corporate Landscapes* (Cambridge, Massachusetts: MIT Press, 2011).

16 Mozingo, 36.

17 Mozingo, 42–43.

18 Mozingo, 43.

19 Harvey G. Flad and Clyde Griffen, *Main Street and Mainframes: Landscape and Social Change in Poughkeepsie* (Albany: State University of New York Press, 2009), 171. This first-rate work presents a concise and compact analysis of the relationship between Poughkeepsie and IBM. It is required reading for any understanding of the Kingston experience.

20 James Passarelli, "IBM and the Westchester Landscape 1945–1975," Master Thesis, Fordham University, 2013, p. 32. This is a full examination of the IBM presence in Westchester.

21 "Watson Inspects IBM Plant Site and Bowlatorium," *Daily Freeman*, May 11, 1954.

22 "IBM Paces Big Expansion in Hurley, Ulster Area," *Daily Freeman*, December 10, 1952.

23 Raymond and May Associates, City of Kingston, New York, *Comprehensive Development Plan*, 1961.

24 Raymond and May, 3.

25 Raymond and May, 12.

26 Raymond and May, 14.

27 Raymond and May, 15.

28 Raymond and May, 15.

29 Raymond and May, 45.

30 David Stebenne, "Thomas J. Watson and the Business-Government Relationship 1933–1956," *Enterprise & Society*, volume 6, number 1, March 2005, pp. 45–75.

31 Emerson W. Pugh, *Building IBM: Shaping an Industry and Its Technology* (Cambridge, Massachusetts: MIT Press, 1995), 146–151.

32 Advertisement, *Daily Freeman*, April 1956.

33 From May of 2013 to January of 2014, the Friends of Historic Kingston sponsored an oral history project, "Kingston—The IBM Years," which completed over fifty interviews of IBM workers and Kingston residents. A series of oral history questionnaires was field-tested in the winter of 2013 and oral history workshops helped prepare the interviewers. Advertisements, newspaper stories, and word of mouth located many narrators eager to record their IBM experience.

34 "Kingston—The IBM Years," The Oral History Project, Interview # 3. These interviews were conducted with an understanding that the names of the narrators (interviewees) would remain confidential. To that end we have substituted numbers in place of names to allow the reader to distinguish one interview from another.

35 William H. Whyte, Jr., *The Organization Man* (Garden City, New York: Doubleday, 1956), 7.

36 "Kingston—The IBM Years," The Oral History Project, Interview # 23.

37 "Kingston—The IBM Years," The Oral History Project, Interview # 5.

38 Watson, 1963, pp. 25–26.

39 "Kingston—The IBM Years," The Oral History Project, Interviews # 32, 46, 43, 29.

40 Watson, 1963, p. 60.

41 "Kingston—The IBM Years," The Oral History Project, Interview # 18.

42 "Kingston—The IBM Years," The Oral History Project, Interview # 39.

43 Watson, 1963, p. 54.

44 Whyte, 305.

45 Whyte, 305.

46 "Kingston—The IBM Years," The Oral History Project, Interview # 12.

47 "Kingston—The IBM Years," The Oral History Project, Interview # 9.

48 Tom J. Watson, *Business and Its Beliefs* (New York: McGraw Hill, 1963).

49 "Kingston—The IBM Years," The Oral History Project, Interview # 38; The dress code applied more strictly to the sales force, while laboratory workers and development staff were less bound by the requirement. Beginning in the nineties, informal dress became acceptable except in upper management where the uniform standard survived.

50 "Kingston—The IBM Years," The Oral History Project, Interview # 49.

51 "Kingston—The IBM Years," The Oral History Project, Interview # 34.

52 "Kingston—The IBM Years," The Oral History Project, Interview # 32.

53 *Town of Ulster Comprehensive Plan*, Town of Ulster, 2007, p. 7.

54 "Bridge Opens over the Hudson," *Daily Freeman*, March 13, 1957.

55 "Kingston—The IBM Years," The Oral History Project, Interview # 34.

56 "Kingston—The IBM Years," The Oral History Project, Interview # 25.

57 "Kingston—The IBM Years," The Oral History Project, Interview # 41.

58 "Kingston—The IBM Years," The Oral History Project, Interview # 43.

59 "Kingston—The IBM Years," The Oral History Project, Interview # 31.

60 "Kingston—The IBM Years," The Oral History Project, Interview # 43.

61 *Town of Ulster Comprehensive Plan*, 2007, 6–7.

62 "Kingston—The IBM Years," The Oral History Project, Interview # 9.

63 "New Shop Center Will Be Erected," *Daily Freeman*, March 29, 1959.

64 Kenneth Jackson, "All the World's a Mall: Reflection on the Social and Economic Consequences of the American Shopping Mall," *American Historical Review*, October 1996, pp. 1117–1121.

65 "Metropolitan Proposed for Area," *Daily Freeman*, October 11, 1956.

66 "Stang Foresees Growth and Progress for City," *Daily Freeman*, December 26, 1957.

67 "Kingston—The IBM Years," The Oral History Project, Interview # 49.

68 "Kingston—The IBM Years," The Oral History Project, Interview # 34.

69 "Kingston—The IBM Years," The Oral History Project, Interview # 13.

70 "Kingston—The IBM Years," The Oral History Project, Interview # 35.

71 "Kingston—The IBM Years," The Oral History Project, Interview # 7.

72 "Kingston—The IBM Years," The Oral History Project, Interview # 19.

73 "Kingston—The IBM Years," The Oral History Project, Interview # 25.

74 "IBM Boosts Restoration of Theater," *Daily Freeman*, February 23, 1995.

75 "Landmark Kingston Men's Store Closing," *Daily Freeman*, January 24, 1995.

76 "Kingston—The IBM Years," The Oral History Project, Interview # 49.

77 "Kingston—The IBM Years," The Oral History Project, Interview # 23.

78 "Temple Emanuel Fund Will Start Drive May 1 for $250,000," *Daily Freeman*, March 20, 1956.

79 "Ulster Land Bought for Catholic Church," *Daily Freeman*, September 25, 1957.

80 Whyte, 405–412.

81 "Drive-in Church to be Held at 9W Theatre," *Daily Freeman*, March 10, 1956.

82 "500 at Drive-in Church Hear 'Happiness' Sermon," *Daily Freeman*, April 1, 1956.

83 "Among the First to Fall at I.B.M.; Thousands in Hudson Valley Told They Are out of Work," *New York Times*, March 31, 1993.

84 "Maximizing Shareholder Value," *Washington Post*, August 26, 2013.

85 "Kingston—The IBM Years," The Oral History Project, Interview # 33.

86 "Kingston—The IBM Years," The Oral History Project, Interview # 49.

87 "Kingston—The IBM Years," The Oral History Project, Interview # 34.

88 "Blood Services Group Says Area Supply Low," *Daily Freeman*, January 26, 1995.

89 "The Town IBM Left Behind," *Businessweek*, September 10, 1995.

90 "The Town IBM Left Behind," *Businessweek*, September 10, 1995.

My Life as an IBMer

By Lowell Thing

I was officially hired on my birthday, March 30th. It was 1969, the end of a decade that had seen flags and draft cards burned in the street, students taking over buildings at Columbia, and John Lindsay as mayor of New York facing down subway, garbage, and several other strikes. As a newsman at WNYC, the city's own radio station, I attended Lindsay's news conferences. I rubbed elbows with people like Gabe Pressman, but I was hardly a member of the city's news-delivering fraternity. Once, after all the major networks had run out of things to ask, I managed to be recognized. I don't remember the question, just Lindsay's answer. It was a disdainful "No." And then the mayor, often described as "patrician," indicated his news conference was at an end.

I decided it was time to find another line of work. I was thirty-two years old, and somehow it seemed like the end of my run in the world of broadcasting. At eleven I had been a child radio actor; I grew up to be a radio announcer. My major at the University of Miami was Radio and Television Broadcasting. After four years in the Air Force, I became a classical music announcer on a station in Coral Gables, and after a year or two migrated to the Big Apple to try for the big time. I worked for a year announcing classical music all day at a station that was located in the Riverside Church. Then I went to work at WNYC on the 25th floor of the Municipal Building where I was for a while a classical music announcer and occasional guest interviewer and then, grabbing the news off the UPI machine, I switched to being the early morning news reader. Occasionally I would take a tape recorder out and cover a strike negotiation or other event. In the crowd of reporters, I held up my microphone and sometimes got in a question to Hubert Humphrey or then-Senator Robert Kennedy or Marshall MacLuhan. When he was a city councilman, Ed Koch would return my phone calls and talk my ears off. I sent audition tapes to the larger news-oriented stations like WCBS and WINS ("All News All the Time") but failed to get a job.

It occurred to me that I had "plateaued." Someone mentioned computers. In 1969 there was still a bit of awe about computers. I signed up for an evening course in programming at NYU, where I remember confusing "jumps" with "do loops." I would probably have dropped out of the course if I hadn't seen an ad in *The New York Times*.

The ad was half of the first page of *The Times*'s Sports Section. It said that IBM was looking for technical writers and no computer experience was required. In later years IBM would hire its technical writers from graduates of specialized college programs; today there are people with PhDs in technical communication. But this was 1969.

I sent in some writing samples and then drove out to a research lab at a place called Mohansic in Westchester County, where I was given a short aptitude test and then interviewed by several very pleasant, almost apologetic technical writing managers. The Mohansic Advanced Systems Division Research Laboratory was surrounded with woods, and the building had a lot of windows with views out into the trees. Down some hallway I passed an experimental industrial robot. Here was a new idea: working in something as interesting as a "laboratory."

So when the letter from IBM arrived with a job offer, I called to accept it. Until I saw the ad in *The New York Times*, I would never, ever have thought of working for a big corporation. On the other hand, the reality of being invited to work for IBM, the world's most famous computer company, was very attractive. I told myself that I could write "that novel" in my spare time. Meanwhile I would be witness to the future. I would be someone with a role in American Industry. Besides, I had a family to support.

The job meant leaving Gotham and moving upstate a hundred miles to Kingston, New York. The group I would work for would work another year in Mohansic and then move to Kingston. But first I would go to Programming School for twelve weeks in a little place outside of Kingston called Port Ewen. The job was contingent on my successfully completing the Programming School. My wife, a girl from Queens that I had married a few years previous, was pregnant with our first child. We loved our rent-controlled apartment in an old brownstone on the Upper West Side of Manhattan, but Kingston seemed like a better place for children to go to school.

I rented a room in the corner tower of an old three-story house near uptown Kingston on St. James Street. I did nothing there but sleep and do homework at night from Monday through Thursday, and drove back to New York to spend weekends with my wife and our future child. On Monday morning I would be back in class in the very functional metal building (later to be owned by Iron Mountain Data Storage) near Port Ewen. In spite of several classes I had attended at NYU, I still did not really understand the difference between a "bit" and a "byte." "Number system" was a concept not revealed to me in elementary or any other school. "Hexadecimal" was a mind-boggler. The instructors were very capable, and by sitting in the first row (at thirty-six I was one of the older students) and raising my hand at the first moment that I didn't understand something, I was able to survive.

In 1969 few computers were yet "interactive." The people who did interact with a computer were called "operators" and they worked in the "glass house," where the large computer or mainframe(s) were located on a raised floor that allowed all the cables to be placed underneath so you didn't have to trip over them. But, for the twelve weeks of Programming School, none of us actually saw the computer. First, given our problem (for example, compute the average temperature for a week given the average daily temperatures), we would sit at a desk and work out the logic of our program and sketch it out using a plastic template that created a flowchart. The flowchart of diamonds (decisions "yes" or "no") and rectangles (processes or simple actions like "Get a daily temperature") showed the sequence of instructions a program would require.

Then we would write each of the sequential instructions (computers still basically operate one logical step at a time) in a programming language. In PL/I, you would first make declarative statements that defined the characteristics of each term you used in subsequent statements. IBM's major mainframe computer was called the System 360 and it read statements in its own language, which was called System 360 Basic Assembler Language.

When we had written our program (a list of individual language statements), we would type each statement on the keyboard of an IBM 029 Card Punch, which would then generate a standard IBM 80-character punched card for each statement. We would then put the cards (they had to be in the right order!) into a box and put them where they would be picked up at the end of the day and taken to the glass house overnight.

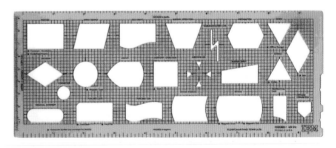

An IBM flowchart template. Courtesy of IBM.

The next morning we found out what happened with our punched cards. Had our program run successfully or not? Chances are it had not and we would find a computer printout that showed exactly what happened when the computer tried to run our program. The printout, or "dump," described the place where the program failed and, by examining the dump in detail (each byte was displayed in the form of two hexadecimal numbers), this information allowed you to debug and correct your program so that it would now, you hoped, run without error and come out with the desired result.

After the twelve weeks at Programming School, I started work at Mohansic, commuting in reverse from our apartment on West 86th Street in Manhattan. I was assigned to a department of technical writers that worked on a product called TSS/360 (for Time Sharing System), a rather advanced version of the System 360 that had a small set of very large customers including GM and a major airline or two. It was IBM's first interactive system. You didn't have to send your programs in as punched cards in boxes. They could be entered and sent in from a terminal. You didn't quite have your own terminal yet; you had to go to a "terminal room," where there was a pool of terminals. On the terminal you could either submit a program after creating it or you could schedule to rerun a program that was already stored in the computer or on a large magnetic tape that could be installed by an operator.

One of the things I learned first was that much work on a product was not the creation of something brand new and original, but rather some kind of update or additional capability that would be added to a hardware or software system in a new version or release. For something like mainframe systems, there might be over twenty new "releases" of the software before it was replaced by something with an entirely new name and set of capabilities. So my first job was simply to write a "Technical Newsletter" for a particular new release of one of the parts of TSS/360 known as the Linkage Editor.

My first manager was an Indian expatriate whose name was Ravi Shukla. Ravi would somehow become a model for my perception of IBM managers I had over the years. They would be unlike other bosses I could remember in my previous work lives. They would basically be more like colleagues, fellow workers whose success was dependent on your success, so they would do everything they could to make your work life pleasant and productive. True, they would have to write an evaluation that would determine how much your next pay increase would be, but that didn't seem unreasonable. Most of the time your manager was just your friend (though you were certainly aware of their status), and sometimes a fellow worker became your manager. IBM also had a policy that in retrospect seems like one of the reasons for their success as a company. People whose value to the enterprise was mainly for their technical expertise or talent, people who often had no aspirations to be a manager, were in general paid at the same scale as their immediate managers. Managing was really seen as another occupation that required certain skills, but not as something inherently hierarchical in terms of value to the company. (Of course, this observation does not quite apply to the very highest levels of the hierarchy.)

From Alan Levy, another early manager, I learned two lessons. Having been a very competent writer himself (he had formerly worked for a major encyclopedia publisher), he noticed that I had been a bit careless in one of my newsletters. I no longer remember the details, but Alan brought this lapse to my attention more as a colleague than as a manager. I was embarrassed to the extent that, although certainly capable of miswriting or misunderstanding something I was writing about, I don't believe I ever again tried to finesse my way through something. It was better to make your mistakes plain and out in the open where others could catch them, than to try to hide them.

The second thing I learned from Alan was something I was already rapidly becoming aware of. Programmers and engineers lived in worlds apart from technical writers. They wrote down "specifications" and handed them over to the technical writers, who basically had to figure out the implications of the specifications for the product's users. Programmers and engineers saw themselves as problem-solvers and were not especially inclined to writing their solutions down in a way that was easy for technical writers to understand. Alan explained an approach he had used as a writer to get a programmer's attention. When the programmer failed to find the time to explain some product details to him, Alan stepped up on his desk and refused to leave until he got the programmer's attention. This was, of course, an extreme approach that I never had to try. Nevertheless,

Emily Thing in front of our first house in Saugerties, 1971. Photograph by the author.

it demonstrated that part of the job of being a technical writer was figuring out how to get the attention you needed from people who would have preferred to move on to the next problem to solve.

My department was moved to Kingston in the winter of 1970, and my wife and I found ourselves looking at a small ranch-style house with two bedrooms in the country north of Saugerties, about a fifteen-minute drive to the Kingston plant and laboratory. We had just enough money for the 10 percent downpayment on a house that we bought for $18,700. (Well, this was forty-four years ago!) There was snow on the ground and, after we bought the house at a bank office closing in Kingston, we drove up to our new and first house that was at that time entirely empty except for wall-to-wall carpeting. We unlocked the door and sat in the dining room (it had an open living room, dining room and kitchen space), leaned against the wall and listened to the silence of being in a little house, our first, in Saugerties, New York, in the middle of winter. The silence was almost, but not quite, absolute; we could still hear the dying echoes of city life on West 86th Street as they faded into our past.

So for the next two years or so, I had, when it wasn't winter, an acre of lawn to mow. We bought the mower, a twenty-six-inch self-propelled one at Sears in the Kingston Plaza near uptown. A shovel and rake and some gardening tools, which we had never had before, we bought at a sort of general store nearby out on Route 32. We brought our first child, Emily, up with us from New York, only two months old, and while we lived in this house, which we would always refer to as "the little yellow house," Suzanne became pregnant with and delivered at Kingston Hospital our second daughter, Hillary. There is a picture in which little Emily and Hillary fresh from baths are being dried off by Suzanne on a kitchen counter.

The house had a small screened-in porch on the southwest corner, and we could see the Catskills from there. Neither of us knew how to name very many flowers when we arrived, but in no time we had learned the names of twenty or thirty. In the spring we would wait anxiously for flowers to come up that we had planted from seeds, flowers that we had never seen before in person—nasturtiums, cleome, cosmos, salvia. A local neighbor, a native of the area, told us about mushroom dirt, the soil full of rotted manure that is left over from the mushroom farm buildings. It could be bought by the truckload. I dug a fifteen-by-twenty-foot hole in the back yard, a foot deep, carted the dense clay soil down to the back, and had the truck driver dump an entire load of mushroom dirt into what became an instantly friable garden. We fertilized it with phosphorus, potassium, and nitrogen, which our local garden expert told us were the three ingredients needed. We grew the usual tomatoes, lettuce, squash, carrots, and some herbs, but also planted some blackberry bushes and asparagus, as well as some new trees elsewhere on the property (some were still there last time we drove by). We were very happy.

It was not absolutely perfect, of course. The water table (never heard of that before) had risen and the basement leaked. Eventually we would get a sump pump, but for quite a while Suzanne sometimes had to wade over to the washer and dryer, fortunately never getting electrocuted. A pipe burst once in the winter just as my parents arrived from Florida to spend Christmas; our next door neighbors, now well into their eighties, shared their bathroom with us until we got the plumbing fixed. Our septic field became exhausted and we had to hire someone to bring us three truckloads full of "bank-run gravel" to create a new one.

Weekdays I drove fifteen minutes to work in the morning and then back at night on a curvy old road called Old King's Highway. Suzanne spent all day with a one-or-less-year-old and a three-or-less-year-old. When I got home at night, I was the popular and more-than-welcome distraction for all three members of my little family. I had become a corporate person, safe in a safe job in a safe company, with a view of the Catskills, a little yellow house, and a beautiful little family. It was difficult not to be happy, and we didn't really try not to be. We went back to the city now and then to visit Suzanne's parents in Queens, but the city had lost its romance or perhaps we had found a new one.

TSS/360 was terminated or eased out, and I was in a group that worked on the Basic Telecommunication Access Method (BTAM) and soon on its replacement, the Virtual Telecommunication Access Method (VTAM). I worked on a guide that showed programmers how to use certain "macro instructions" within a program to communicate with terminals and other input/output devices (and later, but they hadn't arrived yet, with personal computers).

I was finding the work constantly challenging and new at this point. There was always a set schedule and not quite enough time to get as comfortable with the technical aspects of the product as you wished, but in a way this put a certain edge into the job. There was really no time for introspection as in "How do you really like working at a corporation?" And, on a daily basis, your fellow workers, especially the technical writers, were congenial, helpful, collegial, interesting people who worked with you as part of a team. Everyone read books and had a secret hobby or two.

When I had arrived to work full-time in Kingston in 1970, I worked in a building known as "the Lab." Programmers and engineers worked in the "Laboratory." Hardware products were assembled across the street in "the Plant." The original building with a clock on the outside remained the Plant; its very large open areas could easily be modified to fit different assembly lines or test areas. It also housed the main administrative offices, such as those for the plant manager, lawyers, parts purchasers, and so forth. (Over time that side of the street would be expanded to the rear, to the size that you can now see as I write this.) The Laboratory was in a relatively new building across the street from the Plant, and it would also undergo some growth over the next decade or two. For most people who worked at IBM Kingston, if you worked on one side of the street you seldom needed to cross the street for work. The exceptions were after coming back from a trip—to go to the finance office to get reimbursed—or at lunchtime to go to the large cafeteria, which was in the main plant building.

Every programmer or technical writer (my job title was actually "Information Developer"; I retired as an "Advisory Information Developer") had an office, and I believe each one was lockable (though for some reason I don't remember locking or unlocking the office door). Each office had a whiteboard, and it was convenient to have one when having discussions about how something worked. I recall discussions with other writers and with programmers as we tried to understand how a programmer would use VTAM. We had a file cabinet and, after sometime in the early '80s, I believe, we each had our own computer terminal, a 3270. Prior to that time we shared terminals in terminal rooms. Some people kept a very neat office. Some people didn't. From time to time there would be security concerns and we would be urged to lock away specifications and drafts. Almost all documents and drafts related to products or releases in development had to be labeled "IBM Confidential," and there was concern about leaving them lying around in the open.

Whatever your role in developing a product or an enhancement to it, hardware or software, a general step-by-step process was followed, and there was a Development Guide that generally described this process. The first step was to gather "requirements"; that was the job of "product planners" who worked with customers to understand their immediate needs. (Somewhat outside of this process was "research," which could occasionally introduce technological breakthroughs that customers might not have anticipated, although generally there is always a need for "more" and "less costly," general desires that breakthroughs may allow.) Requirements, written down, would then be met by "developers," who would design solutions and describe the new design with a "specification." The specification would become the input to "information development" and other departments such as "human factors," "testers," and "product packagers." Each major step of the way during these phases and during stages of design and development would become the subjects of review and review meetings. Within this process each draft of a publication would also become the subject of a formal review and review meeting.

The details of how these reviews and meetings should be conducted were subject to continual improvements based on both proprietary ideas and industry trends in product development. Something that everyone learned soon enough when working at IBM was that meetings would take a considerable amount of a work day. Actual creation time (in our case, the actual writing) would be only a small part of the work. The manager of the original mainframe System/360 famously proposed that there was a limit on how quickly effective program code could be written for a given project because of the time needed for all involved parties to communicate with each other. You couldn't simply throw more people at a project to get it done sooner or to meet a deadline.

Information development, while important, was never, or at least hardly ever, a critical time cost in product development. Testing often was. Each time you improved an operating system, which is a huge program full of many interdependent parts, you had to make sure that every program that had been changed would work with all existing programs that had not been changed. It was called "regression testing."

For any product, especially for very complex products such as an operating system and its subsystems, there was a need for product support and the ability to fix problems and then get the fixes out to the customers quickly. For many products, especially for larger customers, IBM offered the services, either free or for charge, of "systems engineers" (SEs). Many system engineers reported to work daily at a customer location rather than an IBM location. For hardware, there was a somewhat comparable job known as a "customer engineer" (CE). It was sometimes said that system engineers liked the fact that IBM was not especially known for products that were "easy to use." It was job insurance for the system engineer.

Very soon after we moved into our little yellow house, a colleague and his wife (Dave and Judy Owens) came by and left us some prepared dinners, the kind of gesture that you might expect from people who came from a small town in Pennsylvania and who had met at college and married soon after. Their two sons became the play pals of our two daughters when we exchanged visits. The dropped-off dinners would be the beginning of many social exchanges over the years with the Owens and with other IBMers, most of them technical writers and their families. As I write this, we're in contact with about five or six couples and families we met and became close friends with at IBM.

In 1972 we moved from the little yellow house out in the country to a circa 1898 ten-room house on an older street in Kingston. The main reason for the move was so that our small children would have more playmates. But I think we also felt a bit too remote from shopping and cultural activities. In addition moving gave us a chance to find more space and, since we both liked architecture and the domestic arts, it was a chance to expand those pursuits with all the possibilities a ten-room house could give us. The house was basically in good condition, but the wallpaper and other details needed work. Our new house would give us an ongoing hobby for the next ten years as we tackled one room at a time. But first we started in the hallway, which had a high-beamed ceiling and wainscoting. The house had been built in a center hall Colonial Revival style, and the hallway was especially beautiful. Upstairs and to the attic, we would spend a year working on sanding, repainting and wallpapering the hallway. For the hallway light, we ordered from Philadelphia a brass fixture with two hand-blown sconces. Twice a year we take down the sconces and wash them, and we also shine the brass fixture.

While working on VTAM, I was given the job of writing a BTAM-to-VTAM Conversion Guide. For a year on the book, and for two three-month periods, I worked with two visiting systems engineers who were given the job of providing examples for the book. Gerhardt was a delightful young Austrian who had left his family back home for three months; the other systems engineer was a winning new father who had left his home in California to help out. We had them home to dinner. (The book, however, never happened for reasons that had to do with marketing strategy. One of the frustrating features of working for a large [or, I suppose, even a small] corporation is that only a few individuals can make big decisions.)

I did not usually have a job at IBM that required much travel but, since it was a company in which certain

Moving into the big house in Kingston, 1972. Photograph by the author.

products had parts built at different locations, and also because education courses were often taught at another location, I traveled a few times a year to the plants in Raleigh or Endicott or later Boca Raton, Rochester, Minnesota, and Boulder, Colorado. My favorite trip, in what was perhaps my 15th or 20th year, was to attend a conference in Nice where IBM had a nearby laboratory; I managed to stop off for a weekend in Paris in both directions. For a time I also taught an occasional course about Help Systems at a number of locations, twice at IBM's Hursley plant in Winchester, England (my hotel room window was thirty yards from Winchester Cathedral) and a number of times in Los Gatos, California. For IBM or technical writing conferences or other reasons, I traveled to Seattle, Montreal, Toronto, Chicago, and New York City. Unfortunately I was seldom able to take my wife or family on these trips. Our own vacations were usually in the summer time by car or train to Florida to visit my parents. We did, however, manage to take a month-long family vacation to the British Isles including Ireland when our daughters were ten and eight. I drove my cousin's English sedan all over England, Scotland, Wales and Ireland, staying at farmhouse and city bed-and-breakfasts.

My wife's parents at some point moved to Kingston to be closer to their grandchildren, and my father-in-law taught both of our daughters to swim at the IBM Recreation Center on Kukuk Lane. The pool was crowded on summer weekends but large enough for a crowd, and there was occasional lane swimming. Both daughters learned to swim well. There were softball fields at the recreation center, and employees and their families had the benefit of an organized sports program in softball and volleyball. I who had never played softball in my life found myself at second base. My helpful teammates told me where to position myself in the field. On one occasion someone slid into second base and I managed to hold onto the ball. (The

Emily, Hillary, and Suzanne Thing at the IBM pool, circa 1973. Photograph by the author.

Emily Thing at IBM pool, circa 1973. Photograph by the author.

slider broke his collarbone.) In our attic I still have a trophy from, I think, about 1985. If only I could have learned to hit.

The medical benefits were such that you did not think about it. Our children both arrived totally paid for—or at least the birth part of it. As a vestige of a more paternalistic era when company members still sang songs, IBM sent us a silver spoon when the first baby arrived.

When we lived in Saugerties, I had volunteered to be on a citizen's committee to look into a Town Plan and Zoning Ordinance. In Kingston, within a few years, we were taking our children to the city library (then in the Carnegie Library on Broadway, now part of the high school) and it was almost inevitable that I would help move the books when the library moved to a new location. Later I served on the library board, and for eleven years I was one of two Ulster County residents on the board of the Mid-Hudson Library System. I developed an interest in Kingston's history, especially the history of our particular street and its large old houses. I managed to get the street designated a historic district and served for a time on the city's Landmarks Commission. Sometime in the 1970s, I joined the Friends of Historic Kingston, for which I produced several walking tour guides and served for a time as the group's president. My wife was active in our children's Parent Teacher Organizations and later served as a literacy volunteer. These were personal interests independent of any encouragement at IBM (although IBM did offer small community grants that I sometimes took advantage of on behalf of an organization). I suppose one could say that having a job at a company as stable as IBM enabled many of its employees to make a social investment in the community where they lived.

I perceived that IBM employees could be divided into two groups—those who were willing to work overtime, and those who weren't. Or, to put it another way, people who felt that a certain amount of overtime was "natural" if not obligatory, and those who didn't. In product development (I'm not sure about manufacturing) there were both kinds of people. I believe that, for most people in product development, some amount of overtime would have been needed to get promoted. It wasn't that IBM necessarily encouraged overtime. It was simply the result of the pressure of getting complex products to the marketplace in the desired timeframe. I usually found any new assignment a challenge technically—that is, to learn what I needed to know in order to do my job with great confidence. As a deadline neared for a first or second draft or final publication of something, I often found the need to come into work on weekends. The number of overtime hours wasn't huge, but it did become a rather consistent pattern and even, I suppose for some, a habit. My wife was not all that happy with my need to work overtime, but all in all I think she was very understanding about it.

IBM liked to give awards to people for special achievements, especially after the shipment of a new product or software release, a work effort that might have taken a year or more. An award usually consisted of a handsomely framed certificate and an envelope with a check of a varying size, sometimes a fairly substantial amount. Sometimes the awards would be announced and handed out at a special ceremony in the cafeteria with appropriate words of appreciation. There were actually, although perhaps informally, several classes of award. Late in my career I received a rather major award for some information planning I had done.

After VTAM, I worked on manuals for IBM's new 3270 Information Display System, which replaced the 2260 terminal that we had all used in the TSS/360 terminal rooms. The 3270 was "field-oriented and programmable," meaning that, unlike the 2260, with which data was transmitted character by character, the data (say, an order form) could be sent in streams containing fields or designated character amounts, each with certain rules of display—a much more flexible system and easier for the customer to write programs for. This was in a time when many customers still wrote their own programs rather than buying software packages.

I liked working on the 3270 because it was "real." You could use one yourself. When the unit was shipped, we discovered that simply describing the fields you could program wasn't enough help for the customer. Several systems engineers in Chicago had figured out how to do the programming and, together with another writer, in a week's time we managed to put together a programming guide with examples. I liked going across the street to see where the 3270s were being assembled on something close to a production line. Ultimately the 3270 became corporate-ubiquitous worldwide and, like the mainframe, synonymous with IBM itself. After the arrival of the personal computer in the 1980s, the 3270 began to disappear, but it would take another decade or so.

In the late 1970s I began to work on a new product, an operating system called DPPX (for Distributed Processing Programming Executive) for the 8100 Information System. This was a smaller, somewhat autonomous, computer that was designed to be remotely connected to the larger mainframe so that computing could be distributed more closely to where it was needed. It was a wholly complete system, however, and required its own large set of publications for installation, planning, operation, programming, and maintenance. For this product, at some point, I became the information planner. I took satisfaction in developing and providing the customer with a set of binders to put the publications in, a new idea at the time (although a bit hard to believe now). It seemed to be needed; a set of DPPX and 800 hardware publications could fill a small bookcase!

I believe it was the 3270 that sealed the fate of the secretary at IBM. When I arrived at IBM, there was a secretarial pool that typed up letters, even such interdepartmental letters as invitations to a meeting, from handwritten or roughly typed drafts that we typed on the IBM Selectric, one of which sat on a typewriter stand in virtually every office. It might take a day to get a finished letter back from the secretarial pool (we were always careful to be on good terms with the secretaries). When we had the draft of a document to print out in multiple copies for reviewers, there was a bulk printing facility that we would walk our drafts over to. In time it became more convenient to type letters, memos, and drafts into the 3270, from which copies could be printed out down the hall or by sending something to a faster printer elsewhere. There were always flowers for the secretaries on the annual Secretaries' Day, but eventually there was no one there to send flowers to.

For a while I was loaned out to be a member of the small Information Development staff at the corporate level, reporting to Bill O'Neill, a wry, matter-of-fact but genial, and semi-legendary figure who had seemingly always been IBM's chief representative for its technical writing employees. (IBM was the world's second-largest publisher, second only to the U.S.

Government Printing Office.) I was still in Kingston, but reported to Bill who was in Poughkeepsie when not travelling. I was responsible for formulating and fostering a strategy for information development, and I created a small and rather simple presentation. Strategy point number one, we said, was "Build information into the product." Since IBM had traditionally built products for companies with educated and trained technical staffs, ease-of-use had never been a very high priority, especially for software. (There was a Human Factors or ergonomic department at IBM Kingston, but traditionally it was used mainly for important hardware interfaces and worked more closely with Industrial Design.) At any rate it was one thing to say, "Build information into the product," but the message really had to go to the product marketers who set requirements and the product designers who had to figure out how to build information into the product. Almost anyone who has ever tried to click on "Help" knows that a help index is usually not very helpful. No, the right way to help is to anticipate the need, to be "intuitive." Unlike with Apple, which built a business around the idea, this concept never reached the IBM that I knew, however.

My corporate job lasted eighteen months before I was pulled back to Kingston where I was actually part of the head count. I truly cannot say that I learned a great deal about IBM at the corporate level, although I did travel to some new locations. My one special glimpse into the deepest reaches of the company was when I once visited IBM Research in Yorktown and asked to look at the company's strategy for their five-billion-dollar research investment. Amazingly, they let me look at the document, and it would be no surprise perhaps to anyone to know that back around 1990 about half of IBM's research was for basic problems in astronomy, physics, and special kinds of math. I knew, or had been told, one other fact about "corporate." If you were scheduled

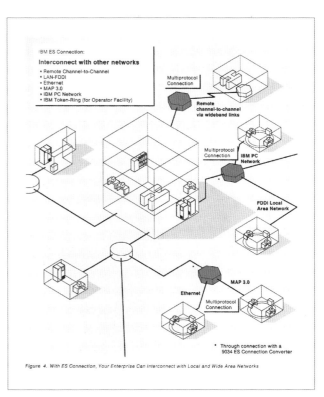

A figure from Introducing Enterprise Systems Connection *that was created (but not drawn) by the author. Courtesy of IBM.*

The cover, designed by John Canevari, from Introducing Enterprise Systems Connection, *an IBM marketing manual. Courtesy of IBM.*

to give a presentation to the board or a special board committee at Armonk, you were told to use flip charts and limit yourself to five charts. When speaking to the top level, it was necessary to be not only succinct, but possibly also a bit reductive.

If I didn't really understand IBM at the corporate level other than what I could glean from reading the glossy Annual Report, I knew just as little about how IBM worked at the highest levels in Kingston. On the one or two occasions when I presented or perhaps was with someone who presented to the Laboratory Director, Roland Pampel, I realized almost immediately that he was very dependent on one or two key assistants and that he was constantly thinking about how what was being presented fit into what were his own immediate and probably very concrete goals. These goals in some mysterious way seemed to be set for him by someone higher in the chain, or perhaps by some set of current rules the company was then following. The lightheartedness quotient in a meeting at this level was very low. And it was perhaps as the result of one of these meetings that I once spent a month (or perhaps it was a week that seemed like a month) with two highly career- or success-oriented people (I was the low man here) that Roland set up as a task force to report back to him about something. I don't remember the problem at all, only the nervous perspiration when we met each morning in a small room.

The legal department had its own office back to the side of the main building, and I recall that getting a legal sign-off on a publication was usually routine unless you needed to point out something new you were doing. In that event you could be pretty sure that you couldn't do it, so it was better not to point it out. About Purchasing and Manufacturing, although I knew where the offices and the test or assembly areas were, I really never learned much in my twenty-seven years there, nor did there seem to be a need to. Everything over there seemed to be humming along—although not much seemed to be happening with mainframes that were being tested; they just stood there with many cables attached. Still, it was a huge building, and its mysterious activities were felt as a presence.

I did learn that head counts and budgets, which were the main result of head counts, were ongoing and important. I sometimes had to help determine the needed head count in various Information Development departments. For an anticipated amount of work, say, a certain number of publications, there would be a needed number of writers, of "heads," expressed in total "man years." A man year multiplied by some overall cost per man year was your department budget. The cost included salary plus benefits and was a ballpark or rule-of-thumb figure—say, $100K per man year. You might add one or two head count for some experimental in-house project. As I recall, your head count was always a bit on the generous side and you could expect it to be cut by a certain percentage.

In about 1992, perhaps a bit earlier, one or two people in IBM got wind of the Internet, which theretofore had been confined to academia and perhaps to a few people at IBM Research. Up until then the Internet's chief uses had been e-mail and data transfer between a relatively small number of Defense Department locations and universities. I remember at around this time attending a lecture at IBM Poughkeepsie by Leonard Kleinrock, who had invented the idea of a network in which data could be sent from one place to another in little packets, each packet possibly traveling a different route through the network, and then all of them being reassembled at their destination. With a whole set of rules about how to manage this, this was, in fact, how the Internet worked (and still does).

There was someone at the corporate level who was going around giving lectures about the Internet that not many people were paying attention to, but I did. The last product I worked on before I retired at the end of 1995 was something quite new for IBM and really an acknowledgement that the world had changed. Several companies such as DEC, Hewlett-Packard, and SGI had come out with a computer much smaller than a mainframe, and these were competing well with IBM's smaller mainframes and distributed systems such as the 8100. These competitors used a computing model or concept known as "client-server." A computer offering services to many users was seen as a server, and individual-user computers were seen as clients. A certain company had developed a user and program command interface that they called UNIX. IBM's customers were demanding that the IT world and its products become standardized, rather than proprietary. They wanted to mix other company's products with IBM's. So IBM changed its long-established mainframe operating system to accept UNIX commands from interactive users and also to run programs built with UNIX program instructions. Soon IBM began to call even its largest business mainframes "servers."

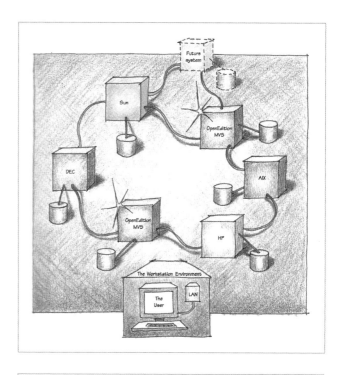

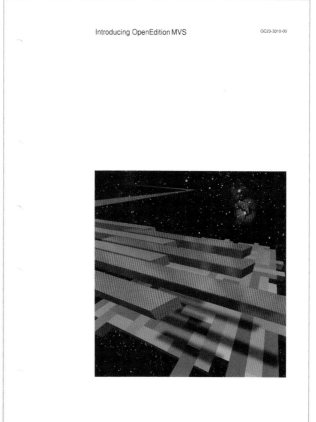

Top right: A figure from Introducing OpenEdition MVS *that was created (but not drawn) by the author. Courtesy of IBM. At right: The cover, designed by John Canevari, from* Introducing OpenEdition MVS, *an IBM marketing manual. Courtesy of IBM.*

The author and family at 55 West Chestnut, 1989. Photograph courtesy of the author.

I wrote the marketing publication that explained this new idea, and I got the feeling that my primary audience was not customers, but IBMers. And once we began to think in terms of networks, the Internet seemed more visible. We learned that we could let customers download electronic copies of our publications (using the File Transfer Protocol, or FTP).

Shortly after that, a university in Minnesota invented Gopher, which allowed anyone with access to the Internet to have a text-only hierarchical view of files (books, documents, papers, etc.) available for reading from a certain location. And a short time later came something truly transcendent—the World Wide Web and its browser, Mosaic. This was about 1993. Only a few years earlier, I had attended a lecture by the inventor of the term "hypertext," Ted Nelson. Ted had been, in a way, the prophet who, without anyone actually understanding it or believing it, had predicted the Web. His ideas were about pure types of hypertext, all kinds of hypertext that to this day have not yet been invented. When the Web emerged through the ideas of Tim Berners-Lee, the actuality of its version of hypertext obscured Nelson's ideas. Nelson almost immediately became a historical figure.

In my last role at IBM, I created the first, or perhaps one of the first (it would be hard to know), IBM Web sites for the new UNIX version of IBM's Enterprise System/370. When I started, there were no design rules, but by the time I finished IBM had latched onto the Web and had a

Kingston—The IBM Years

corporate design structure promulgated from on high. In my spare time, I became an enthusiast of a Web that I almost felt I had invented (I believe most of its earliest discovers felt that way; it was like being the only one in your neighborhood who knew the Secret of the Future—and this was the day of the 56K US Robotic modem!) It was easy to create a simple Web site with HTML 1.0, and I quickly put together a Web site for the City of Kingston with the help of one of my daughters, an artist and graphic designer. With a few other non-IBM enthusiasts, I went around to the local Kiwanis and other places telling them about this new world and finding that as yet the world was still asleep. But gradually it woke up.

It was somewhere around this time (1993, I believe) when IBM changed as a company to work for, when the policy of "safe employment" (my term) was implicitly disavowed. I don't recall the details of how the word came down, but suddenly it was there. Some people would have to be let go. It wasn't an abstraction. A day came when our managers went into a room that I can't imagine and were told to prepare a list, and another day when they were told how many. In my department we felt lucky to lose only one of our colleagues and, though we liked her (we were, after all, a team), she had not been in the department very long. It was both sad and unbelievable. Of course, any sensible person would realize that any company, especially with quarterly earnings goals, might someday have to "downsize," but IBM people in general had been lulled into a sense of security. I remember how we not only felt sorry for our colleague, but for our manager who had to deliver the message. We felt sorry for ourselves and for the world. Now, if you magnify this scene to the size of the installation and the entire company, you can see that it was a transformative moment, not only for IBM but for America (that our proud nation could no longer have a company that never let anyone go).

There was a moment when it seemed like it was all over for IBM, but its new CEO, Lou Gerstner, changed everything. He came to Kingston, and probably went to every other IBM site in his plane or helicopter, and talked to everyone in the cafeteria without notes, answering everyone's questions with great businesslike adroitness. He told everyone that he had discovered the answer to IBM's problems. "We have to listen to the customers," he said. That idea seemed to be turning things around.

But not for IBM Kingston. A year or two later it was announced that the Kingston plant was closing, but with most of our jobs simply being moved to IBM Poughkeepsie. Somehow I think I lost track, or was just never aware, of how much this cost Kingston in terms of population. Most, if not all, of my IBM friends and colleagues simply had a longer drive each day but continued to live in Kingston. Of course, it meant that no new jobs would be coming to Kingston and that, as IBM people retired, some taking inducements to retire early, their incomes might be reduced and their jobs would not be filled by new Kingston residents. I car-pooled with a fellow information developer, Jim Steipp, a friend of many years. We liked to argue politics a lot. We also managed to take turns reading Milton's *Paradise Lost* on the way to our new work location.

I retired on the first day of 1996, having in my spare time already started a Web site that I would work on for another ten years. I did go back to work part-time for a short while as an independent contractor, long enough to notice that working for IBM was no longer the same.

It is only recently that I've begun to realize, especially considering today's job market and the new economics in which many young people are having to create their own jobs, that those who worked for IBM Kingston were in an unusually lucky time and place. ⊙

Lowell Thing was an Information Developer (technical writer) at IBM for twenty-seven years. He is a former president of the Friends of Historic Kingston and spearheaded the drive for state and national recognition of the Chestnut Street Historic District in Kingston. His forthcoming book The Street That Built a City *is a history of Chestnut Street and its influential 19th- and 20th-century residents.*

IBM, Then and Now

By Hugh Reynolds

IBM represented what in time might be considered the last "industrial age" for the greater Kingston area. First there was agriculture, then coal, bluestone and cement, then for a while garment factories, then IBM.

As in many things, IBM's coming to Kingston was a combination of opportunity, luck and timing, or so said a former city water superintendent.

I dropped by the water department on a slow news day to find Superintendent Ed Cloonan in a nostalgic mood. IBM, at the time—around 1970—was in one of its expansion modes. There were some concerns about adequate water supply for the new buildings they were planning, thus my visit.

Cloonan told an interesting story.

About a year before IBM's advance men (in those days) came to town, Cloonan was paid a visit by another team from another major manufacturer. They were interested in building a new plant. They'd needed at least 200 acres, which Kingston didn't have, and at least a million gallons of potable water a day, which Kingston had in abundance.

The Kingston water system, connecting Cooper Lake in the town of Woodstock to the city via the town of Ulster, had been established in the 1890s. Expanding to meet a growing city's needs, it had not been professionally surveyed in years. Cloonan, seizing the opportunity,

Cooper Lake, Kingston Reservoir. Photograph by Kitty Sheehan.

Chilled water pipes at IBM Kingston plant. Courtesy of John F. Matthews.

convinced the ultra-conservative water board to approve an engineering study of the entire system, one designed to accurately gauge capacity and delivery systems. It took about a year and produced a state-of-the-art, up-to-date document.

The impetus for the survey went elsewhere, but a year later an IBM advance team paid a call on the superintendent. They were looking to locate a plant and they needed proof of adequate water supply.

Cloonan told me he went to his filing cabinet and pulled out the voluminous engineering report. The team flipped through the report, expressed their admiration for the department's attention to detail and, impressed, asked if they could borrow it overnight. "You guys are really on the ball," Cloonan said they told him.

The terms were reasonable to both parties. Kingston would supply the company's Town of Ulster complex with up to 1 million gallons of water a day (which they rarely used) at agreed-to premium prices. All necessary connections to the existing water system would be paid for and maintained by IBM.

The ensuing construction boom was not confined to the 280 acres the plant occupied in Lake Katrine.

Witness the major public construction that took place circa 1954–94.

The Thruway was completed in the mid-'50s with exits at Kingston, New Paltz and Saugerties. Rte. 84, the Kingston-Rhinecliff Bridge and the Newburgh-Beacon Bridge were all completed within 15 years of IBM's arrival.

The Kingston school system was consolidated in 1959, followed by the construction within five years of seven new schools. Schools were also built in Onteora, Saugerties, Rosendale, Esopus and Red Hook.

Ulster Community College was created; SUNY–New Paltz expanded.

The county office building and a new city hall were constructed.

Both Kingston hospitals underwent major expansions, with IBM as a generous contributor.

Kingston Plaza was followed by massive regional shopping malls in the Town of Ulster.

Kingston-Ulster airport expanded.

Middle-income housing sprang up in Whittier, Rolling Meadows, Barclay Heights, Tillson and Red Hook.

Kingston-Rhinecliff Bridge under construction. Courtesy of John F. Matthews.

Kingston-Rhinecliff Bridge, 1957. Photograph by David Hermeyer.

Some of this would have taken place without IBM, but all of it?

IBM's was a paternal culture. It is interesting to note that, on IBM job applications, one of the last questions asked if the applicant had a relative working for IBM.

The company took care of its people, and that loyalty was reciprocated. IBMers had their own country club, traveled together on company-sponsored trips, participated in company social events, athletic leagues. The company cafeteria offered good food at good prices. The company had its own security and fire fighting forces.

While the company hired most of its workforce locally, it also infused the population with outside talent. It offered opportunity to

advance within its system. It recognized and encouraged community involvement by its employees. It employed local tradesmen and artisans whenever possible. And it rarely quibbled about the price of things.

IBMers, homegrown products for the most part, were of the community, deeply involved in most of its affairs, but separate. The "loaned executive" program helped many a nonprofit, United Way for the most part, reorganize, recruit volunteers and reach goals.

Plant security was the byword, the rule, and for good reason. IBM Kingston began by making computers for the government, principally the defense department. It was called FSD for Federal Systems Division.

I once asked a friend of mine who had a "good job" at IBM,

At top: IBM Kingston badge. Courtesy of Bruce Whistance. Above: IBM Kingston cafeteria. Courtesy of John F. Matthews.

exactly what he did. He had some kind of title like production engineer expeditor. "To tell you the truth," he said, "I'm not exactly sure and when I begin to figure it out, they transfer me to another department."

Employees wore badges with their photos, names and department emblazoned thereon. Visitors were rarely out of the sight of their company escorts.

There were jokes about IBM standing for "I've Been Moved," but in most cases a transfer was a requirement for promotion. There, too, the company took care of its people. Market value on homes of those transferred was guaranteed, a significant boost to the local real estate industry.

IBM liked to project itself as a "good neighbor." It was located on Neighborhood Road, after all. It paid its taxes without protest, creating something of a tax haven in the Town of Ulster. The company did not get involved with local controversies, though its employees were encouraged toward civic activity, including holding public office. Two mayors of Kingston were IBMers.

IBM left Kingston in 1994 but, as with most things with IBM, the planning for the move started many years earlier.

Here's a story.

In late 1985, WTZA opened its studio in Kingston at 721 Broadway. It was a gala event, much like a Hollywood premiere, with all the town's leading lights in attendance. Gov. Mario Cuomo was guest of honor.

The Great Orator, speaking in his extemporaneous style, offered a few platitudes on why a new television station linking the Hudson Valley from the Tappan Zee Bridge to Albany (thus TZA) was important to the economic and cultural growth of the region.

He concluded by speaking of a meeting he had had recently at IBM headquarters in Armonk with company CEO Jack Akers. Akers, some may recall, was the IBM executive who did not have a computer in his office.

"From the CEO's office in Armonk, you can see Connecticut, perhaps 500 yards away," Cuomo said (and I'm writing from memory here). "I asked him if his company had any plans to move across the border." Akers's response, the governor said, was "IBM has no plans to move out of Kingston."

The collective gasp at this "good news" was as if something had sucked all the air out of the room. That IBM had even *thought* about moving from Kingston was unthinkable, unimaginable.

It being close to my 11 PM deadline, I rushed back to the paper to file my story. The headline read, "IBM says it has no plans to leave Kingston." One can only imagine the reactions around kitchen tables and diners the next morning, not to mention at IBM.

An IBM public relations man called me shortly after I arrived for work around 8:30 the next day.

"What kind of journalism do you practice over there?" he demanded. "You write a story about IBM and you don't call IBM for comment?"

"For one thing," I told him, "you guys are all gone by 5 PM. I was writing at 10:30. More importantly, when the governor of the state makes a statement in front of 250 people, we take it to the bank."

Mollified, but hardly satisfied, he offered me his private number to call "any time, day or night, anytime you write anything about IBM." He did not reiterate that IBM had no plans to move out of Kingston.

IBM employment peaked in Kingston at about 7,100 workers in 1988. (At the time, the county had a work-force of about 60,000.) These were among the best, most secure jobs. I think it's fair to calculate that at $40,000 per job, plus another $10,000 in benefits, IBM was generating some $400 million in annual payroll at its peak. Economic development specialists tell us the multiplier effect of manufacturing is on the order of almost two to one, meaning the financial impact approached a billion dollars a year.

But IBM's impact over a 40-year period on this region was much more than that. The company offered good wages in an area notorious for sweatshops. It was only about two generations removed from the advent of IBM when local workers were paid less than a dollar a day, while owners and managers resided in million-dollar mansions (adjusted for inflation) on hills overlooking the waterways. Was it no wonder, then, the company's location to this area was so strenuously opposed by local Brahmins?

A few days after IBM formally announced it was closing its Kingston plant—after years of pointed

Floor of Kingston shirt factory. Collection of Friends of Historic Kingston.

denial—Lt. Gov. Stan Lundine came to town. "It will take time," he said to a group of glum-looking local officials.

I think the media and, by extension, the community, was dismayed by the duplicity surrounding IBM's departure from Kingston, given its perceived "open door policy" for so many decades. I don't think anyone connected systematic downsizing with eventual closure. Certainly, nobody in government was talking about IBM leaving. IBM continually used the term "right-sizing" in response to such inquiries. Up to a year of the closing, most notably at a chamber of commerce breakfast, IBM spokesmen were denying any plans to leave Kingston. Of course, the "right size" (ultimately, zero) was never apparent until the moving trucks literally pulled up to the curb.

IBM has been gone for almost 20 years now. Foiled in the hope that a so-called "state-of-the-art" manufacturing plant would soon attract another major employer, the community has pursued a policy of diversity.

There is nostalgia about the IBM days when jobs were plentiful, businesses thrived, opportunities abounded, and restaurants were full, an appreciation made all the more poignant by what the community has become without its main benefactor.

The relationship between IBM and local media was formal, professional and on IBM's terms. Typically, we would get press releases on this or that event, promotions, new products, community contributions, executive comings and goings. Releases always featured an 8 × 10

Publicity shot of Clarence (Bud) Howe, general manager of IBM Kingston, with baby.

glossy of the subject. It was all very professional and very carefully controlled.

TAX HAVEN?—With IBM as its main taxpayer—this was prior to the arrival of mega-malls—Ulster, like the town of Olive (with the reservoirs), was seen as a tax haven. I mentioned "tax haven" in regard to Ulster in one of my late '70s columns, after which I got an angry phone call from a town resident. We compared properties. Bottom line, as a city resident I was paying almost twice the property tax as an Ulster resident on a similar property.

TAX ON THE RICH?—Around 1990, just as the first round of retirement incentives were being rolled out, I got a phone call from an IBMer protesting the so-called "Cuomo tax on the rich."

This man, who seemed the typical retiree—he said he was in his mid-50s, had worked for IBM for 32 years, earned $50,000 as an engineer—said he had been offered a retirement package that included almost three years salary, unused vacation and sick pay, etc., in total over $150,000. A few years prior, the state enacted a 2% surcharge on all adjusted salaries above $100,000.

"I've never made $100,000 a year," the man protested. "This isn't fair."

"It sounds like the state is taxing you $1,000 on the additional $50,000 (above the minimum), which for most people probably sounds like a good deal. I'll do the story if you'll allow the use of your name," I told him.

He hung up.

PRANKSTERS—IBMers were considered a breed apart, especially at their workplaces. One of my favorite IBM stories, which we didn't print, was about the Beemer who bought a new Volkswagen from a Kingston dealer. He was forever bragging to coworkers about the gas mileage, etc., until a few pranksters in his department came up with an ingenuous scheme.

While the VW guy was at lunch, they snuck out into the parking lot and poured gas into his tank. Mr. VW, who checked his mileage every day, noticed immediately. "I'm getting 40 miles a gallon," he claimed. Then 50, then 60.

They allowed him this euphoria for a week or two, then began siphoning gas from the car. Mileage dropped to 30, 15, 10. Mr. VW was back to the dealer on an almost daily basis. Dealership mechanics couldn't figure it out. They had every part of that car spread out on the repair shop floor. VW was besides himself, until pranksters confessed. ☉

Hugh Reynolds has been a working journalist in Ulster County for more than 40 years, first with the daily newspaper and later as a publisher of a weekly newspaper. He is currently a columnist/reporter employed by Kingston-based Ulster Publishing, which publishes the weekly newspapers in Woodstock, New Paltz, Saugerties and Kingston. Like many of a certain age in the region, he comes from an IBM family. His mother and her siblings were IBMers, as were two uncles by marriage. They were of the generation that first worked at "the plants" in Kingston and Poughkeepsie. Hugh Reynolds worked briefly at IBM Poughkeepsie as a contract employee before entering the field of journalism.

Ulster County Ghosts

By Gail Godwin
Illustrations by Frances Halsband

Preface

Before Frances Halsband and I started work on "Ulster County Ghosts," we took a trip down 209 to Stone Ridge one October afternoon. We wandered about the grounds of the old house at the corner of Schoonmaker Lane and Pine Bush Road and I told stories about the three years (1973–1976) Robert Starer and I had lived here and pointed out the rooms where each of us had worked. The house had been through several owners since then, and somebody along the way had pointed up the stonework and put on a nice new metal roof. However, the grounds had been neglected; the beautiful stone terrace below the house was in ruins; old trees had died and been left standing; formal plantings had been obscured by weeds.

In 1985 I published *The Finishing School*, inspired by this house and this hamlet (which I named "Clove" in my novel) and by the layers of society Robert and I mingled with while living in Stone Ridge. There were the farmers and the merchants, there were the old families who

IBM and the Kingston-Rhinecliff Bridge

could trace themselves back to the Huguenots and first Dutch settlers, there were the affluent weekenders and, most recently of all, there were the IBM families. All these social elements found their way into my story and shaped the fates of the characters in Clove.

After a lunch break at the Egg's Nest in High Falls, Frances and I doubled back on 209 and took the Enterprise Road exit to the former IBM plant, remarking on the irony of the name change. When this place had been a world-class enterprise, the road running through it had been called Neighborhood Road. There was no lack of parking space in the vast empty lots. It was a Saturday and, after pressing our beseeching faces against the entrance to the main building, a young security guard materialized out of the shadows and said he could allow us to look at the lobby, "but please don't blow anything up." He permitted Frances to take a photo of the huge aerial view of the IBM plant which still hung on the back wall. I told him the story of how, in the IBM days, you had needed to get a "gold coin" from the receptionist in order to release yourself from the visitors' parking lot.

It is not always that you finish a project and realize it has left you with an even more beguiling question than the unknowns that made you want to take on your project in the first place. My question lies in Frances's eerie drawing of the "ghost" plant superimposed against the land around it like a giant animal settling into the landscape. What happens to such a place and its people when the giant creature gets up, shakes itself off, and goes away?

 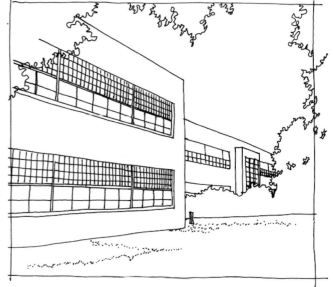

Kingston IBM buildings 2013

Ulster County Ghosts

i. The House

In 1973, Robert Starer and I, after running up a thousand-dollar phone bill between Iowa City and New York City and exchanging several hundred letters in one year, rented a house in Stone Ridge, New York, to test whether our tempestuous spirits could make a life under the same roof. I was a writer of fiction who required a moat of space and quiet around me during working hours. The University of Iowa, surrounded by countryside, had suited my temperament and might have continued to if I had not met Robert one summer at the Yaddo artists retreat in Saratoga Springs, New York. A composer who taught at Juilliard and Brooklyn College four days a week, Robert needed to be in driving distance from New York City.

The Stone Ridge house, built in the late 1770s of the same fieldstone of the ridge on which the Marbletown hamlet sits, began to live in us the moment we saw it from the road. Our realtor, Dorothy King Vanderburgh, was driving us down Schoonmaker Lane toward Pine Bush Road when it appeared before us on the far side of a field of waving grasses. Robert later told me I gasped "Is *that* it?" He had felt the same way. Neither of us had lived in such a house or in such a landscape. Until the age of fourteen, Robert had lived in Vienna. From his bedroom he could watch the daily passing of the Orient Express. I had grown up on a residential street in Asheville, North Carolina. Afterwards for both of us, it was cities: Jerusalem, Miami, London, New York, Iowa City.

Dorothy took us though the empty rooms and showed us how it had grown from a small farmhouse (a kitchen and a room above) to its present oblong two-story size. She sketched for us the social history of this very small (5.2 square miles) and old hamlet: the Dutch patroon farmers, the French Huguenots, the British colonists, the eighteenth and nineteenth-century farmers and merchants, followed by the summer visitors and later weekenders, arriving in twentieth-century trains and automobiles—and most recently the influx of IBM employees when the Kingston plant was opened in 1955. Our present landlord was the young president of a national consortium of department stores who had been transferred to California. He had bought this house as a weekend retreat only a few years before and couldn't bring himself to sell it yet. His name was Allen Questrom, but locals continued to refer to the house as "the Davenport House," and that is what we would call it when we needed snow plowing or plumbing repairs.

"We're at the corner of Schoonmaker Lane and Pine Bush Road …"

"Now let's see, that would be—"

"The Davenport house."

"Oh, the *Davenport* house." The voice got friendlier and we were told someone would be over right away. (I later learned from Bill Davenport that before it was "the Davenport house," it had been known as "the Gordon house," where his grandmother, Sarah Gordon Davenport, had been born.)

Dorothy informed us that Mr. Questrom had provided us with a caretaker who lived just across the field and would take care of our grounds and small repairs. His name was Ernest Howard and he had recently retired from the Kingston IBM plant. I knew very little about IBM at the time, other than I wanted an IBM typewriter when I could afford one and that an avant-garde colleague in the Iowa Writers Workshop wrote his lecture notes on IBM computer cards, which everyone thought very cool.

From then on, we were to hear a lot more about IBM, both from villagers' talk and from Ernie's IBM stories, told to me when he was painting or raking leaves, stories which ranged from awe and gratitude to insider humor, both the remembered and the mythologized kind.

Old Mr. Watson, the founder, liked to drop in at the new Kingston plant. One day he was inspecting the men's room and an employee came in, used the facilities, and started to leave. "Wait, young fellow," said Mr. Watson. "Can't you read what that sign says?" "Sure I can read, Sir," the young man told him. "It says, 'Employees must wash hands before returning to work,' but, you see, I'm not returning to work, I'm going to lunch."

The overall impression we got was that IBM was the rather feudal and paternalistic latest layer of the area's many levels of local history which had brought a much-needed business boom to the area. If you were with IBM, you could expect instant smiles from doctors' receptionists and bank tellers upon presenting your "Big Blue" credentials. You were as good as paid for—in advance. Some locals resented this; others reassessed their skills and rushed to the new Kingston plant to put in job applications. Ernest Howard was among these.

"The day Ernie was hired by IBM he felt he had died and gone to heaven," Mrs. Howard told us when she invited us for tea shortly after we had moved into the Stone Ridge house.

We signed the rental agreement in Dorothy's office in March of 1973 and I returned to Iowa City to finish my semester of teaching before packing up my worldly goods and driving back east in May. But, having seen the house, we were already imagining ourselves working in the rooms we had each chosen for ourselves, having our drinks down on the stone terrace overlooking the fields and the Mohonk tower above, and eating dinner by candlelight in the large formal dining room. Allen Questrom had left us his long oak dining table and four dining chairs, which he later sold to us for $25. Aside from that, we began with nothing except our books, and two plastic lawn chairs.

Robert worked downstairs in a room off the dining room. It looked out on the back lawn and the fields, but he faced the wall because he could not work with a view. He had rented a grand piano and bench for $10 a month from a local lady who no longer had the space but wanted to keep it for her grandchild. I worked upstairs facing fields and the tower of Mohonk (I like a view) on a desk bought for $15 from a High Falls antiques dealer. The first novel I finished in that house was *The Odd Woman*, my third novel, set in an academic community inspired both by Iowa City and Urbana, Illinois, where I held a postgraduate fellowship in 1971–1972.

I also began writing musings and stories inspired by this old house and the noises at night. Some came from inside the walls, mysterious little knockings and scratchings; others from outside. One night I was wakened by someone banging frantically on the front door. I called down from the window to ask who was there. "Do you have horses ma'am?" cried a man's voice. "There's horses all over the road!" I looked out and sure enough, there was a cluster of horses standing in a moonlit Pine Bush Road as though they were in a painting. After this I wrote a story called "Dream Children," about a woman who rides her horse recklessly in the fields "because she had nothing to lose," and who discovers (as I did) that when she is alone during the week she can lie in her bed and float about the house in a sort of waking dream and see the landscape as it was hundreds of years ago. She also finds a ghost child living in the

The Davenport House in Stone Ridge

upstairs storage room. Later, some Canadians made a TV film based on the story, but failed to capture its full ghostly dimension. They relied too much on special effects and too little on possible reaches of human consciousness.

On Mrs. Heisenbuttel's grand piano, Robert began by writing his second set of *Sketches in Color*. He told me he wanted to start with something small and undemanding since he was not accustomed to having another person overhearing him compose. A decade before, he had written seven highly successful teaching pieces for piano: "Purple," "Shades of Blue," "Black and White," "Bright Orange," "Grey," "Pink," and "Crimson." And now, warily, with an eaves-dropper on the floor above, he embarked on "Maroon," then "Aluminum" (that unromantic title, announced at supper, chilled me a little), then "Silver and Gold" (slightly more romantic, though with hints of aging), then "Khaki" (was he feeling regimented?), then "Pepper and Salt" (was domesticity getting to him?), then "Aquamarine" (an upbeat piece in quintuple time), and lastly "Chrome Yellow," which he described as "non-symmetrical rhythms set in symmetrically-shaped phrases." (A comment on the current state of our relationship?)

After he had satisfied himself that my upstairs proximity had not jinxed his muse, he accepted a commission for a "large work for brass," which he titled "Stone Ridge Set." Immediately following its completion came a call from Martha Graham. Could Robert have music ready for her dance company's 1974 spring recital? She had an idea for a new work to be called "Holy Jungle," a fantasia based on Hieronymus Bosch's triptych, "The Garden of Earthly Delights."

Robert's excitement to be working with Martha again was infectious and off we went to the nearby Ulster County Community College library to lug home books about Bosch. When I try to describe that library to people today, they think I am exaggerating. A community college? A relatively *new* community college? But 1973 was before the days of budget cuts and the downsizing of liberal arts. Lavish art and architecture books crammed the shelves. There was every current magazine and scholarly journal you could wish for, as well as the *Guardian* and the *Times Literary Supplement* from England. All the latest novels and new nonfiction were in a special section, the McNaughton collection. There was also a sumptuous assortment of classical music scores and Robert would check out Bach or Debussy or Mozart, depending on the day's mood, to play for us that evening on Mrs. Heisenbuttel's piano.

Robert had previously composed the music for four Martha Graham works: "Visionary Recital" (which later became "Sampson Agonistes"), "The Lady of the House of Sleep," "Secular Games," and "Phaedra," which became the Indian Summer triumph of Graham's final performing years. The new piece, "Holy Jungle," would be danced by others—Martha, 79, had stopped dancing at 76—but she wanted music from Robert to evoke a "pilgrim's journey through the labyrinth of temptation."

He worked passionately at his rented piano, no longer self-conscious about being overheard. Dancer and composer talked on the phone, he went to see her in the city: he was in a state of creative ecstasy. "When I collaborate with Martha," he told me, "it is like a love affair of the mind." He had a file folder of Martha's typed work-notes to him during their previous collaborations and when he let me read them I felt as though he were sharing something as precious as love letters. I was amazed and touched by the humility and uncertainty with which she approached her work.

These are ideas, perhaps good and perhaps not so good and surely open to change …
It is difficult for me not to be distressed with it now. It all sounds so stilted and undanced. Please understand.

About "Visionary Recital," first performed under that title, later changed to "Sampson Agonistes," she wrote to Robert:

I have used this as a working title. It may turn out to be permanent but it will have to wait until we are both in the work […] it means the inner debate each of us engages in, and the scenes and actions do not belong to any particular time in history or even legend, nor to any specific place. Each of us carries in himself the Image of his own world and projects it into a more or less coherent universe, which becomes the stage on which his destiny is played out.

"No wonder the Jungian analysts flock to her performances," said Robert.

I still keep that folder of work-notes close by, to give me courage when I'm doubting my unfinished projects. *It's all right not to know,* the notes reassure me, *that's why you feel compelled to write it.*

After Robert's 1974 collaboration with Martha Graham on "Holy Jungle" and the good review in *The New York Times* by Clive Barnes ("The score by Robert Starer emerges like skeins or veils of music. It hangs in the air, not supporting the choreography too much physically, but setting moods and rhythms and suggesting the aural décor and space that Miss Graham required …"), Robert received a bunch of commissions and so it came about that while we were still in the house in Stone Ridge, we collaborated on our first of what would be many musical works over the course of our next twenty-seven years together. Our collaborations began on an afternoon walk when I complained about a story, "Indulgences," that just was not jelling. There was a promiscuous modern woman, a costume designer, who couldn't fall in love, and an apocryphal tale of a fourth-century saint, Pelagia, a courtesan who gave up her wild life and her many costumes for God. I couldn't make the two connect. But Robert said he heard an opening already: Pelagia, swaggering through Antioch with her maid, reciting (like Don Juan) her list of lovers. I found that working with a composer was like playing a game: all the stress was removed. Who remembers the name of librettists? "The Last Lover," a chamber opera for woodwind and soprano, mezzo-soprano and baritone, became a lively work with theological overtones and was premiered at the 1975 Caramoor Festival in Katonah. It was to become one of our most popular works, performed in New York City, Brooklyn, the Maverick in Woodstock, Music in the Mountains at New Paltz, and in churches and concert halls around the country.

We ended up renting the Stone Ridge house for three years, during which time we wrote many pieces of music and fiction, both separately and together, within its old walls.

ii. The People

The Old Guard

Dorothy Vanderburgh dropped in on us often. I think she felt protective of us. She became a sort of fairy godmother. She and I shared a birth date, and the three of us had a little party in mid-June of 1973. She was turning 80, I was turning 36. She had been taken aback when she first saw our two orange plastic lawn chairs in the living room and two old horsehair pillows we had taken off a rotting wood chaise to use as a coffee table. The following day she sent down two comfortable armchairs, a mahogany coffee table, and two floor lamps "so both of you can read at the same time."

While Robert was away during the week, Dorothy often invited me for supper at her house at the top of Buck Road. She froze casseroles twelve at a time, and served the meals on fine table-cloths fully laid out with silver and china. A long-time member of Stone Ridge society, she knew everybody's story and the story behind that story. "This place was one big party before the War. Barn dances, picnics, dinner parties—of course we had servants then. During the War we had our Bundles for Britain at the Grange meetings, but things were never really so lively again." Dorothy had a repertoire of sentimental poems and tear-jerker songs from old melodramas; if encouraged, she would render verse after verse in her high, ethereal voice.

> *Many a young girl I have saved*
> *From a dark and watery grave*
> *While walking the streets*
> *At night on the job …*
>
> *A tear, a sigh; alas, goodbye!*
> *The pardon came too late …*

She could sing all the verses of "The Fatal Wedding."

The wedding bells were ringing on a moonlit winter's night
The church was decorated, all within was gay and bright.
A woman with a baby came and saw the lights aglow,
She thought of how those same bells chimed for her three years ago …

right down to:

The husband died by his own hand, before the break of day!
No wedding feast was spread that night, two graves were made next day …

Later I would draw on these evenings at Dorothy's for my novel *Violet Clay*, in which the diminutive octogenarian realtor, Minerva Means, presides over her late father's mountain retreat, enchanting guests with her elegant tableware, local gossip, and spooky lyrics sung in a high, ethereal voice.

On occasion, Dorothy's old friend General Sherman Hasbrouck would cut through the woods separating their houses and join us after dinner. He was born in 1898 and loved to tell how as a boy he would walk cross-country for days at a time, stopping at Catskill farms to ask for food and a squirt of cow's milk. He graduated from West Point and served as Commanding General of the 97th Infantry Division in World War II. A few years younger than Dorothy, he was to outlive her and give the elegy at her funeral. He remarried in his early nineties and lived until the age of 104, becoming one of those rare humans who get to inhabit three centuries.

The Farmers

There were farmers to the left of us, all the way to the end of Pine Bush Road, where a Dutch Patroon farm was still in full operation, from cattle to crops. In the other direction, halfway down Schoonmaker Lane, Mr. Stevens had his horse farm. It became my favorite afternoon walk, in all weathers, and I often caught him in conversation with the horses: "Get back! Behave! Come on, girls. Get up, old (inaudible). Cold today!" (to me).

Daisy and Earl Osterhoudt, who raised dairy cattle, also owned Stone Ridge Liquors, set back on a little rise between the drug store and the library. During a single weekend in the spring of 1975, they lost four cows to a mysterious disease. "When a cow runs a high fever, 106, her ears turn real cold and her body real hot," Daisy explained, packaging up my *Mouton Cadet*. "When I went out last night, the last one was groaning and breathing hard, but when she looked at me she seemed to get better. Then she stopped breathing and that was it. I said to my husband, 'Have you ever actually watched a cow die?' He said, 'No, I don't believe I have.' One that went had just been bred, but she hadn't freshened yet. And then those two little heifers! We are about half-crazy."

Ernest Howard: neighbor, caretaker, IBMer

It was a shame Robert didn't like a view when he was working, because the window of his ground floor studio made a perfect frame for what we came to call "Ernie's lawn." This pristine swath of emerald grass our caretaker pampered with an old-fashioned push mower in summer and started raking free of leaves as soon as they began to fall. At the far end of this lawn, separating it from a steep rock wall and the field beyond, was a white picket fence that mirrored his white picket fence on the far side of the field. It seemed that when he was not repainting his fence he was repainting ours, and this was when we had our most sustained conversations. Dorothy Vanderburgh's specialties had been social history and gossip. Ernie's were local lore, how things worked, and IBM. He proudly admitted not "going down" to New York City in "a quarter of a century," but he was a trove of information about Stone Ridge customs. People had "always" dropped off unwanted kittens at that corner, he told us after we found a tiny orange creature shrieking from an old tree in our yard. "Everybody knew" a cat would find a home somewhere along Schoonmaker Lane or Pine Bush Road. If a farmer didn't welcome it as a mouser, the Newkirk sisters in the old stone house next to ours could be counted on to feed it till it crossed the fields to a better life.

Ernie was 66 when we met him in 1973; he had been hired by IBM when he was already in his forties. His story about the opening of the Kingston-Rhinecliff Bridge in 1957 gave me the shivers.

> *"Before we had the bridge, see, you had to cross the river by ferry. When the river froze, the ferry couldn't run, so you had to go all the way down to Poughkeepsie to cross. The official opening of the Kingston-Rhinecliff Bridge was scheduled for May, but as a convenience to IBM workers it opened for traffic in February, while the river was still frozen. The only thing was, there were no guardrails yet. They had to wait until it was warm enough to pour cement."*
>
> *"You mean, they drove across with no guardrails?"*
>
> *"Sure. They were eager to get to work. It was fine, as long as you didn't look down. You and Robert drive across that bridge all the time. How many times have you hit the guardrail?"*

"Oh, I was in maintenance," was how he cavalierly described his job at the Kingston plant, which I took at the time to mean something lowly, but then in 1983, when I was researching my IBM character Eric Mott for *The Finishing School*, I saw with the help of on-site historian Bob Jagoda at the Kingston plant, how widely the word "maintenance" could be applied. We learn towards the end of *The Finishing School* that Eric Mott, the IBM father of the heroine's cousin, maintained the vacuum tubes of an enormous computer being readied in Kingston for the military.

> *"It was a top secret job … top secret … see, we had two identical systems trading off every twenty-four hours. Every day it was my job to go over those tubes. If one gave*

out, I had to replace it. We had to replace
about five hundred tubes every month."
— Eric Mott in *The Finishing School* (1985)

I never did find out what Ernest Howard's actual job was, but it seemed to me that he would have been the perfect maintainer of those top secret tubes.

The last big project Ernie did for our landlord was to put in a drainage system on some additional property Questrom had bought across the road. First Ernie found out where the water was coming from, then he put in drains and a pump. As a final touch he built a pump house and finished it off as beautifully as if he were planning to house a beloved dog there.

Ernest died unexpectedly in January of 1976 of a heart attack. "When that doctor came out and said he was gone, I'm sorry to say I used a certain expletive for the first time in my life," Mrs. Howard told us. Dorothy Vanderburgh drove Robert and me to the funeral. Dorothy was cordial but chilly. We had just done the unforgiveable—bought a house in Woodstock from *another realtor*—though eventually she forgave us. Ernest Howard was buried in Woodstock with his forbears, and Robert and I (and the orange cat that had been dropped off at our corner) moved to Woodstock five months later. "Hi, Ernie," we got in the habit of saying whenever we passed the town cemetery on Rock City Road.

iii. The Ghosts

Ghosts, those people and places in our lives that aren't there anymore but refuse to go away, are best honored when we make a home to enclose and protect them. Novelists are used to doing this. You take a very old stone house whose stairs you still climb in your dreams and you put in some people, maybe not based on any people who ever lived there, not the Gordons or the Davenports or the Questroms or the Godstars (as Robert Starer and I liked to refer to ourselves) but some people named DeVane, whose Huguenot ancestors arrived in Ulster County in the late seventeenth century. These DeVanes, proud but fallen by the 1950s, are a brother and sister, in middle age. Julian DeVane, a failed concert pianist, supports them by teaching music lessons to children. Things are looking better since IBM brought an influx of money—and children—and Ursula hopes they won't have to sell off any more DeVane land to their neighbor, the horse breeder, Abel Cristiana.

Enter a fourteen-year-old girl, Justin Stokes, whose widowed mother has uprooted them from Virginia to join the Ulster County household of Aunt Mona Mott, just separated from her IBM husband Eric Mott, and her inscrutable little daughter, Becky. The Motts won't divorce because Eric Mott couldn't bear to have

it known at family-oriented IBM, and because Mona and Becky would lose all their benefits. It is summer, and the homesick, friendless Justin escapes down a country road on her bicycle and soon she'll be meeting Ursula and her brother Julian, who will draw her into their world with all its ghosts and some dangerous family secrets.

Walking in the Stone Ridge fields with Robert one afternoon in 1974, I said, "I want to write a deep country dream of a novel, with surrounding fields like these, and there will be haunting music coming from an old house."

"Oh, what kind of music?" he asked, his composer's ear alerted.

"Oh, I don't know. Something that would spook a passerby. Maybe eleven cellos playing at the same time."

"*That* would be a very unusual sound," said Robert.

I later abandoned the eleven cellos and settled for a single grand piano inside an old stone house.

In 1983, when I was researching my IBM character Eric Mott, whose over-scrupulous caretaking of everything and everybody is pivotal to the tragic outcome, I made an appointment with the on-site IBM historian, Bob Jagoda. On the telephone he told me to park in the lot outside the Kingston plant. Our interview turned out to be so productive that I incorporated Bob into the character of Eric Mott, who later becomes the on-site historian when the adult Justin visits him at work and learns the rest of the story in which she was implicated. Here is Justin's description of the Kingston plant in its heyday:

> Neighborhood Road looked like a movie set, though whether for a euphemistic document about a friendly corporation or a surrealist's sinister satire on corporate life it was hard to say. I tended to the latter impression as I drove slowly down the neat-straight road (lanes carefully marked for left turns) with smooth grounds and office buildings on both sides. I made a left turn into the parking lot beside the big white building with the American flag in front (Mott's headquarters) and a mechanical arm swung up to admit my car after I had pressed a button. A sign directly above the button informed me that the only way I could get out of the parking lot was by depositing a special "gold coin" (available only from the receptionist at the main desk) into the slot at the exit gate. Employees with earnest, abstract faces walked briskly from one building to another, tiny replicas of these faces flapping with the identification tags on their lapels. After I had identified myself to the stylish middle-aged receptionist at the main desk and had explained my purpose, and she had confirmed this by a phone call to Mott's secretary, I was given a visitor's badge, with a picture of the building I was now in, but with azaleas blooming all around it. The receptionist, who looked as if she had just come from the hairdresser, wrote my name in an even, legible hand, and watched me while I pinned it on my sweater. I could tell she was having trouble "placing" me, and I tried to soothe her cautious imagination by chatting briefly about the weather. I was glad I had worn a skirt for this outing. By the time she had issued me my "gold coin" for getting out of the parking lot later, the atmosphere of the place had begun to make me feel like an outlaw disguised as a kind niece, come to pay dutiful respects to an old uncle at his place of work. I sat down next to a window behind which two uniformed guards kept surveillance over a bank of closed-circuit monitors. On the monitors, you could watch the movements of employees as they went from room to room in the inner recesses of this building. While waiting for Mott, I followed the stoop-shouldered man with dark hair and a small moustache. Down one hall he went, coattails flopping behind him on the black-and-white monitor. Then through a door and down another hall. He reminded me a little of Charlie Chaplin. Then the door to the reception room opened and there stood the same man in living color. He stared at me, trying to decide something.
>
> "Justin, honey?"

It's a mesmerizing occupation, this assembling and reassembling of ghosts. I never tire of it. You can preserve a parking lot in its magical/sinister era (when it required a "gold coin" to get out!) from its future incarnation when grass from the old farmland days will once again burst through its cracked and empty acreage. You can bring back the dead, hear their voices, reassess their place in your overall design, and even find new jobs for them. ⊙

Kingston IBM parking lot 2013

Gail Godwin is the author of fifteen novels, the most recent being Flora *(2013).*
The Finishing School (1985) was set in Ulster County. Her memoir, Publishing, *comes out in early 2015. She lives in Woodstock, N.Y.*

Frances Halsband is an architect and founding partner of Kliment Halsband
Architects in New York City. She is a long-time weekend resident of Wood-
stock. Frances has illustrated two books by Gail Godwin: Evenings at Five
and Publishing.

IBM Comes to Kingston, The Colonial City

By William B. Rhoads

During Kingston's era of IBM-fueled prosperity (c. 1955 to 1993), much new construction followed generic modern design—design free of obvious quotations from past styles—as commonly adopted by architects and their clients around the United States. However, because Kingston had long taken pride in its colonial history and old stone houses, there remained a strongly held belief that Kingston was "the colonial city." Moreover, as the city had supported a distinguished contingent of Colonial Revival architects in the first half of the twentieth century, their influence encouraged the continued use of Colonial design for the colonial city, despite the growing authority of modernism in American architecture as a whole.

Kingston's foremost architects from 1900 into the 1940s were Myron S. Teller (1875–1959) and Charles S. Keefe (1876–1946), both dedicated to Colonial Revival design. Keefe admired Colonial architecture as "typically American," and he could not fathom why architectural journals pushed modern houses when none of his residential clients wanted modern, impractical, "square boxes." His death in 1946 spared him from the sight of the apparent triumph of modernism in the American architecture of the 1950s and '60s. Teller, a friendly rival of Keefe, also could not abide the rise of modernism, which became more and more obvious after his withdrawal from active practice in the 1940s. Teller's grandson recalled: "he detested Frank Lloyd Wright and most other styles of modern architecture. I remember being with him in Kingston as we drove by a modern public school building. 'It looks more like a factory than a school!' he exclaimed."[1]

In 1926 Teller formed a partnership with Harry Halverson (1891–1988), who also was a proficient Colonial Revivalist in the 1930s. However, by 1960 Halverson was willing to adopt the modern idiom for some commissions, notably schools including, perhaps, the school that so upset Teller. In the late 1940s and early 1950s, just before the arrival of IBM, Halverson's preferred mode for school and commercial buildings was a stripped version of the Colonial and of classicism where ornament was much reduced in what seemed a compromise with orthodox modernism's complete rejection of historical ornament. This compromise is evident in Halverson's George Washington School (1950) and Rondout National Bank (1952–53) on Broadway at Henry Street, as well as the Homeseeker's Savings & Loan Association (1955–57; fig. 1) at 235 Fair Street from early in the IBM era.[2] The bank retained severely simplified classical pilasters, quoins, and frieze on the Broadway façade while the main banking room had old-fashioned (and somewhat incongruously informal) knotty pine trim. The savings and loan façade was even more Spartan, with barren brick walls to either side of the central entrance, which was framed in classical marble but had no prominent classical moldings.

Fig. 1. Homeseeker's Savings & Loan Association. Photograph of Halverson rendering, Friends of Historic Kingston (FHK).

It was into this architectural environment that IBM in 1953 announced its acquisition of farmland in the Town of Ulster and the next year began construction of steel-framed, brick-faced offices and a manufacturing facility far larger than anything Kingston and Ulster County had known in the past. Twenty years earlier, IBM had adopted the Colonial Revival for its red-brick engineering laboratory building (1930–33, by New York architect Charles H. Higgins; fig. 2) with classical entrance portico and Colonial cupola in Endicott, New York, but its more recent buildings in Poughkeepsie had avoided the Colonial Revival or any overtly historical style. In Kingston, the first phase of construction included the Administration Building, designed by Louis Rossetti, an architect in the Detroit engineering firm of Giffels & Vallet, Inc. Rossetti had a great deal of experience designing large industrial

Fig. 2. IBM Laboratory, Endicott. Postcard, collection of William B. Rhoads (WBR).

facilities, having been a draftsman in the 1920s with the firm of Albert Kahn, Inc., renowned for its Detroit automobile plants. By 1949, when associated with Giffels & Vallet, he planned General Electric's Electronic Headquarters Group in Syracuse, a design comparable to IBM Kingston.[3]

The Administration Building (figs. 3, 5), still a distinctive landmark on Enterprise Drive, resembles Building 002 of Poughkeepsie's IBM plant, which had opened in 1948 with Dwight Eisenhower and Eleanor Roosevelt present at the dedication. In Kingston, the central entrance of the long façade was marked by a projecting pavilion and the large, bold letters, "IBM" (now removed), which in September 1955 were lifted atop the strictly rectangular pavilion (fig. 4). This pavilion bore only slight traces of its classical ancestry—its broad surface of stone gave it a certain monumentality, and the central grid of doorway and windows was articulated by a severely geometric stone frame. The IBM sign replaced a classical pediment, and sculpture gave way to a clock where numbers (too complex in form) yielded to twelve dashes. An early architectural rendering shows the vertical rectangle of the Administration Building's central pavilion played off against the long horizontal ranks of windows (with bands of glass blocks above clear glass) of the

Fig. 3. IBM Administration Building, Kingston. Photograph of rendering, FHK.

Left: Fig. 4. IBM sign installed on the Administration Building. Photograph, FHK. Above: Fig. 5. Former Administration Building in 2013. Photograph 2013 by Stephen Benson.

two-story, brick office section and vast one-story, brick sections of the manufacturing plant. Without the IBM sign the complex could have been mistaken for a school, as Teller complained, except for its enormous scale; the plant, dedicated by Thomas J. Watson, Jr., on November 2, 1956, included two manufacturing buildings (one for the Military Products Division, which made "giant computers that are the heart of SAGE, the nation's early-air-warning system," the other for the Electric Typewriter Division), each 1,000 by 250 feet. Together with the other buildings, this meant that the total area of buildings on the site was about 787,000 square feet.[4]

Subsequent buildings for the IBM complex—the two-story, concrete-and-glass Engineering Laboratory (1958; fig. 6) and its four-story addition (1968), the latter, at least, by architects Wank, Adams, and Slavin—were surfaced with white horizontal panel walls (not the yellowish brick of the earlier Administration Building) alternating with recessed bands of windows. Here the pure white surfaces of modernism triumphed not only over any trace of classical ornament but also over Rossetti's fussy brickwork and glass blocks. It seems that

IBM fully embraced modernism in the 1960s when leading modern architects designed buildings for IBM—Eero Saarinen the Thomas J. Watson Research Center (1961) in Yorktown Heights, Marcel Breuer the La Gaude Laboratory (1962) in France, and Skidmore, Owings & Merrill the corporate headquarters (1964) in Armonk.[5]

Kingston IBM's growth accompanied and helped foster new construction in the city and county. The *Kingston Daily Freeman* in its year-end assessment of 1966, concluded that the year saw "the biggest building boom in the history of Ulster County and the Kingston area." IBM itself planned a 150,000-square-foot warehouse, while the area saw new housing, schools, commercial and hospital buildings, motels, and places of worship.[6] (It must be said, however, that some of the new construction resulted from destruction wrought by urban renewal of Broadway East in Rondout and the demise of the historic post office in Midtown.)

IBM projected an image of modernity, rejecting any obvious signs of historical quotations or revivals, as was appropriate for the forward-looking, inventive enterprise. However, it does not seem that IBM employees

Fig. 6. IBM Engineering Laboratory, 1958. Photograph, FHK.

Kingston—The IBM Years

were any more attracted to modern houses than were other homeowners in the area. Gavin A. Cullen, Robert P. Crago, and Richard J. Whalen, general managers of the IBM plant in the 1950s and early '60s, all bought conventional houses in well-established neighborhoods. Cullen in 1956 resided at 262 Manor Ave., a Tudor Revival house built in 1930; Crago in 1957 resided at 249 Pearl St., a 1940 Colonial Revival house designed by Augustus Schrowang; and Whalen bought a ranch house in Hurley in 1955, before becoming general manager. Architect Robert Milliken suggests that IBM employees who expected to move within a few years to other IBM sites tended to buy existing houses rather than go through the process of building new.[7]

Still, the thousands of IBM employees, many new to the area, required new housing, and housing developments rose on the outskirts of Kingston and the rural areas of nearby towns. Novelists Anthony Robinson and Gail Godwin treated the split-levels and ranches as not-very-welcome intruders upon the countryside. Robinson had grown up as part of the Maverick colony outside Woodstock and deeply admired its founder, the writer, printer, and dreamer Hervey White, as well as the community of artists, writers, and performers that White gathered around him in his utterly simple housing for nearly forty years until his death in 1944. In Robinson's 1969 novel, *Home Again, Home Again*, the Maverick colony (renamed Rawson Colony) has a new neighbor, the Rawson Park subdivision, made up of IBM families (IBM thinly disguised as "Morrissey-Lowe" with a plant in "Kingsley-on-Hudson") whose cars, 217 houses, and way of life upset the protagonist, a writer whose links to the colony resemble Robinson's. In marked contrast to the bohemian eccentricity and rusticity of the colony, suited to artists in a rural setting, the Morrissey-Lowe houses are conventional, with mass-produced components and suited to the striving middle class anywhere in America: "Virtually all were sided with pastel-tinted aluminum and garnished here and there with brick or stone ... lending weight to the structures and thus keeping them anchored to their

concrete slabs during windstorms. Almost every house had a two-car garage attached to it which added greatly to the over-all size of the building, making the homes appear grander than they were." Unwelcome as this development was, far worse was the scheme (contrived by a dastardly general manager) to acquire Rawson Colony and turn it into the site of a Morrissey-Lowe laboratory with adjacent employee recreational parkland.[8] In fact, while a housing development did arise near the center of the Maverick colony, IBM did not create a facility on Maverick land.

Godwin in her novel, *The Finishing School* (1984), describes Lucas Meadows, eight miles from Kingston, where "the beautiful meadows had been plowed up, its hundred-year-old trees cut down to make way for several dozen 'split-level' houses, all alike in the treeless sunlight except for their colors. Every third house was light yellow ... . The two in between, light blue and light tan. ... [T]hese houses had been designed to hold what was, statistically, the average modern American family ... two adults and two and a half children." Godwin's teenage protagonist, Justin, is "bothered" by "their lack of history" (she grew up in the history-laden South and was drawn to an old stone house near Lucas Meadows) and even more by the fact "that they seemed designed to make everybody as alike as possible." The inhabitants, "interlopers" in the long-settled community, were in Godwin's telling remarkably alike, most fathers working at IBM Kingston, the mothers dutifully performing standard household routines, including placing a lamp with cellophane-covered shade in the living-room picture window. When Justin returns to Lucas Meadows some twenty-six years later, it was no longer a "prairie of uniformity." Trees had "grown up around the houses. Different homeowners ... declared their personal tastes" by adding garden ornaments and sheds, changing the color schemes, and eliminating most of the lamps in the picture windows. "Perversely," the adult Justin missed the "neatness" and "purity" of the "houses and lawns seeking to blend themselves into an anonymous little enclave of upscale democracy."[9]

In actuality, a number of IBM employees chose to buy old homes in well-established Kingston neighborhoods and so did not fit Robinson's and Godwin's stereotype. John L. Weber, an engineer, and his wife Antonette acquired an early stone house on Green Street that had been restored by Myron Teller in 1920. Lowell and Suzanne Thing purchased and preserved a handsome c. 1900 Colonial Revival house at 55 West Chestnut Street. Lowell was a technical writer for IBM and is one of the city's leaders in historic preservation. In nearby Hurley the historically important, eighteenth-century Van Deusen House was purchased in 1969 by Jonathan Oseas, an IBM programmer, and his wife Iris, a Kingston native who has long operated Van Deusen House Antiques with her husband. These examples contrast with the IBM families portrayed in Godwin's novel who care little about history and spurn an old stone house for not having enough closets and bathrooms.[10] Still, Godwin doubtless accurately described IBM workers as mostly welcoming the idea of owning and occupying a new house in a development of similar new houses not far from their jobs.

Such was to be the appeal of Whittier Estates, ambitiously planned in 1955–56 as a small city in the Town of Ulster, just north of the new Kingston-Rhinecliff Bridge. Masterplanned, Inc., developers from Long Island, envisioned a community of some 3,000 or 4,000 houses with its own water and sewage systems, shopping center, library, and hospital. A number of the farms purchased by the developers had remained in family hands since before the Revolution, and *The New York Times* reported that "several houses with historic value will be preserved as points of interest for visitors." Whittier was to attract IBM home-seekers and so was strategically located near the 300-acre IBM Recreation Center built by the company for its employees. The Recreation Center offered a swimming pool, playgrounds, sports facili-

ties, and picnic areas, not unlike the employee park in Anthony Robinson's novel. Whittier's model homes rose on Kukuk Lane, adjoining the Recreation Center. Ads in the *Freeman* in 1957 (fig. 7) touted Whittier's "Montclair Wonder Home" with four bedrooms and two pastel ceramic tile baths at $14,250. "Other Whittier Wonder Homes starting with 'The Salisbury' at $12,750" were also on display. However, the developer failed to meet deadlines in completing houses that had been ordered; in March 1957 only twenty-five families were occupying their homes, while sixty-nine houses remained unfinished. Distressed purchasers formed the Whittier Home Improvement Association. The developer ran into financial difficulty and, in actuality, Whittier consisted of only a cluster of nearly identical houses just east of Route 32 on Vestal Hills Drive and connecting streets, as well as the model houses on Kukuk Lane. The standard Whittier house (fig. 8) resembled a Cape Cod cottage of the early twentieth century, but with no obvious Colonial details. In a general way the Whittier houses resembled the thousands of "semi-modern style" houses erected

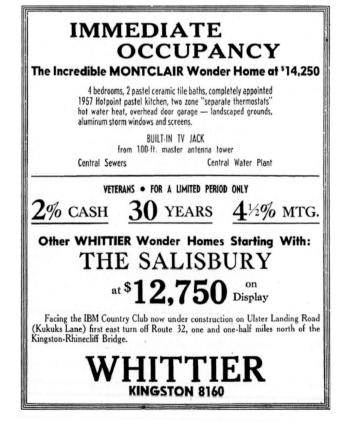

Fig 7. Whittier Wonder Homes advertisement, Kingston Daily Freeman (KDF) May 31, 1957.

Fig. 8. A Whittier Home in 2013: 54 Meadowbrook Drive. Photograph 2013 by Stephen Benson.

beginning in 1949 at Levittown on Long Island.[11] At Whittier the street front consisted of an attached garage, a large living-room window, doorway, and low bedroom windows tucked under the eaves. Bricks faced the bedroom section and continued as a wall a few feet to the side of the house, while bricks also projected below the bedroom windows to support a flower box. As at Godwin's Lucas Meadows, owners have, over the years, individualized their homes and lawns.

The model houses on Kukuk Lane included one (at 98 Kukuk Lane; fig. 9) of the standard type just described, but also three larger and more expensive ranch houses. One of these (120 Kukuk Lane) soon became the home of Arnold and Jayne Pettingill, whose family came to include several IBMers. The Pettingill's ranch house had been designed in 1955 by Herman H. York of Jamaica, New York, according to blueprints (fig. 10) remaining at the house. York, who probably designed other Whittier homes, was described in *The New York Times* as "one of the more prolific architects of development houses in the East," having planned houses for some 75,000 families from Massachusetts to Alabama, although his practice

Fig. 9. 98 Kukuk Lane. Photograph 2013 by Stephen Benson.

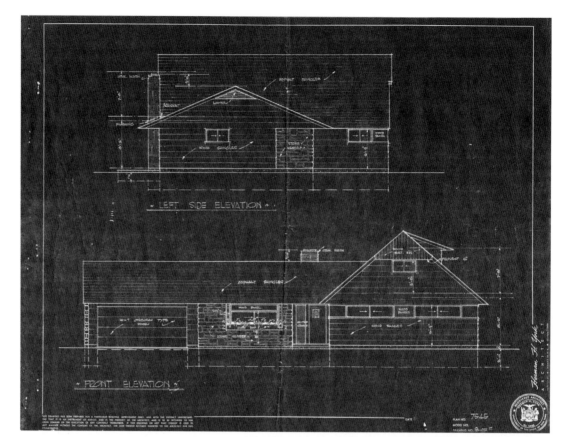

Fig. 10.
Pettingill
House, 120
Kukuk Lane,
front elevation.
Blueprint
courtesy
of Gaynel
Tavares.

Fig. 11.
Drawing
inspired by
Pettingill
House, on
endpaper
of 1965
Saugerties
High School
Year Book.
Courtesy
of Gaynel
Tavares.

At top left: Fig. 12. 160 Griffin Drive, Rolling Meadows. At left: Fig. 13. 115 Griffin Drive, Rolling Meadows. Above: Fig. 14. 4 Norma Court, Hillside Acres, the home of IBMer Robert P. Winrow and his wife Dorothy. Photographs 2013 by Stephen Benson.

was centered on Long Island. The Pettingill house, following York's Plan No. 7545, would be larger and with finer features than the standard Whittier house. York called for wood-shingle siding accented with sections of stone veneer and, by the front door, "fluted glass." Attached was a two-car garage; standard Whittier homes had one-car garages. The Pettingills enjoyed a flagstone entranceway, stone fireplace, radiant heat, and an open floor plan—no partition separated dining and living rooms. York placed the dining and living rooms at the rear of the house, and the stainless-steel kitchen at the front where it could function as a "living kitchen ... a control center for daytime activity."

Children living on Kukuk Lane attended Saugerties schools. One of the Pettingills' daughters, now Gaynel Tavares, graduated from Saugerties High School in 1965, and her year book has a full page sponsored by IBM titled "Progress," where "education" is described as "an unending search for knowledge." As Tavares points out, the year book was organized around the theme "As Architecture Develops So Does Education" and pictures an old stone house on the cover, while a sketch (fig. 11), based on the design of the Pettingill house, graces the endpapers and represents progress beyond the Colonial house type.[12]

Other developments catering to IBMers included a wider range of house types than found at Whittier's main cluster. At Rolling Meadows, in the Town of Hurley but near the city, 160 Griffin Drive (1958; fig. 12) is a ranch house with Colonial touches, while 115 Griffin Drive (1956; fig. 13) suggests a late and simplified version of early-twentieth-century prairie houses. Hillside Acres (fig. 14), developed by William Zang, bridges the City of Kingston–Town of Ulster border. Zang advertised in 1964 that "all homes in the tract shall be custom designed and custom built and in almost any style

Fig. 15. DeJoy House, 32 Lynette Boulevard. Photograph 2013 by Stephen Benson.

and design with a promise of no duplications." This neighborhood bears some resemblance to one described in Godwin's novel, where an IBM manager (better paid than Lucas Meadows fathers) "bought a spacious ranch-style brick house on the outskirts of Kingston. It had elaborate landscaping and central air-conditioning, and ... [a] pool, glowing like a large blue jewel."[13]

Among Hillside Acres' impressive, architect-designed houses is the residence (fig. 15) of John DeJoy, an IBM manager and ultimately a director, at 32 Lynette Boulevard. Altogether modern but avoiding the austerity of the glass box, the DeJoy house has a rich variety of stone and wood planes, and striking projections in the broad carport and the steep copper-roofed family room. DeJoy had joined IBM in 1955, worked in the assembly line, and was made a manager in 1967. Two years later, Pratt-trained architect Edmond G. Loedy planned the house, which is still owned and occupied by the DeJoys. In high school, John DeJoy had considered a career in architecture, and he has long been interested in art and photography. When commissioning the design for his own house, he knew he wanted something modern, not Colonial. He was attracted to a modern house by Loedy in Hyde Park that was owned by an IBMer, Phil Cerniglia. Loedy, now practicing in Millbrook, describes himself

as "a creative architect, visionary," who in 1978 proposed radically transforming the Poughkeepsie Railroad Bridge by adding shops, hotels, restaurants, and condominiums while maintaining trains powered by "magnetic levitation." Although proud of his home designed by Loedy, DeJoy points out that the Tennessee marble and vertical boards surfacing the home were opposed by the architect, who rejected stone that was not "functional" and who preferred horizontal boards. Over the years, DeJoy has enjoyed planning a patio and pool on the south side of the house, doing much of the labor himself. For the family room (added 1999) with its dramatic copper roof and skylight, DeJoy happily worked with architect Nancy Copley (d. 2013) whose own remarkable house in Accord, combining organic and geometric forms, he admired and visited.[14]

The Colonial Revival remained a choice for home builders at Hillside Acres. Harry Halverson's residence (1957; fig. 16) for Kirtland Snyder, an attorney, at 30 Overlook Drive resembles a ranch house with prominent two-car garage, but it is fitted with Colonial trim, and the sloping site allowed a full two stories at the rear. Snyder was not an IBMer, but no conclusion can be drawn linking modern houses to IBM employees, since two of the most distinctive modern houses in Hillside Acres were also built for non-IBMers. The Abelove House (1958; fig. 17) at 49 Ringtop Road, described by *The New York Times* as "an uncharacteristically modern Hudson Valley house [that] exudes all the futuristic optimism of 'The Jetsons'" (an animated sitcom first aired on ABC-TV in 1962–63), was the creation of William H. Van Benschoten (1910–1968) for Robert Abelove, a businessman, and his wife Anne. Trained in architecture at Yale in the 1930s, Van Benschoten in the 1950s and '60s maintained his office at Vinecroft (c. 1884), a Queen Anne–style country house developed on the Hudson at West Park by his grandfather, for whom the architect was named. The Abelove house, like Vinecroft, is an inventive design, but in place of the late-nineteenth-century picturesque there

is a bold, rectilinear, glassy shaft, raised up on brick piers and thrusting out horizontally from the hillside. George and Jane Jetson and their Space Age family of 2062 could almost be at home here. Almost, but not quite, because Van Benschoten was in fact designing a serious example of sophisticated modern architecture. The long rectilinear shaft, and especially the gently sloping, V-shaped or butterfly roof, relate to "The House in the Museum Garden" (1948–49) by noted architect Marcel Breuer for exhibition at the Museum of Modern Art. This exhibition house was seen by thousands in 1949 and influenced subsequent American middle-class housing. Van Benschoten was commissioned by Dr. Abraham Feldman, related by marriage to the Abeloves and an admirer of their home, to design

Fig. 16. Snyder House, 30 Overlook Drive. Photograph 2013 by Stephen Benson.

Fig. 17. Abelove House, 49 Ringtop Road. Photograph 2013 by Stephen Benson.

Fig. 18. Feldman House, 40 Lynette Boulevard. Photograph 2013 by Stephen Benson.

his more earth-bound, but still glass-walled house (1963; fig. 18) at 40 Lynette Boulevard. The Feldman house also incorporates a butterfly roof. (A similar roof marked the Imperial 400 Motel [1964–66; demolished] at 615 Broadway, part of a California-based chain.)[15]

Communities east of the Hudson River also furnished housing for hundreds of Kingston IBM employees. Construction of the Kingston-Rhinecliff Bridge, designed by Dr. David B. Steinman, "World's Famous Bridge Builder," began in 1954, and it opened for traffic in 1957. Two years later, when the highway was completed connecting the bridge and Route 9W near the IBM plant, the plant's general manager, Richard J. Whalen, told attendees at the ribbon-cutting that the roadway would "enhance the Kingston area's position as the business, financial and shopping center of Ulster, Northern Dutchess and Southern Columbia County." At the same event, the chairman of the State Bridge Authority felt obliged to explain that the bridge had not been built to serve the IBM plant, but "the other way around"—the bridge and its access road were simply among the existing or assured advantages encouraging IBM to locate where it did. Harry Halverson

had designed the bridge's toll booths and administration building (fig. 19) in 1956, the latter in the stripped classical style he also chose for banks at the time.[16]

But where would IBMers and their neighbors go to shop? Stores continued in business in the shopping district of Uptown Kingston on Wall and North Front Streets, but new shopping centers with spacious parking lots increasingly drew away customers. Ulster Shopping Center opened in 1962 on Albany Avenue Extension, just over the city line in the Town of Ulster and convenient to the IBM plant. The developers and builders of this shopping center had erected others on Long Island and in Brooklyn. The corporation's president, Harold Lewis, boasted in December 1961 that Ulster Shopping Center would be "the only truly modern shopping center in the trading area, although others have been discussed and projected." "Modern" was the appropriate term to describe the three main stores—Woolworth's, Food Fair, and Wallace's (fig. 20). Food Fair, however, advertised its supermarket as "ultra-modern." The new, 144-foot-long Park Diner (1963; fig. 21) at 37 Albany Avenue, manufactured in five sections by Paramount Dining Cars

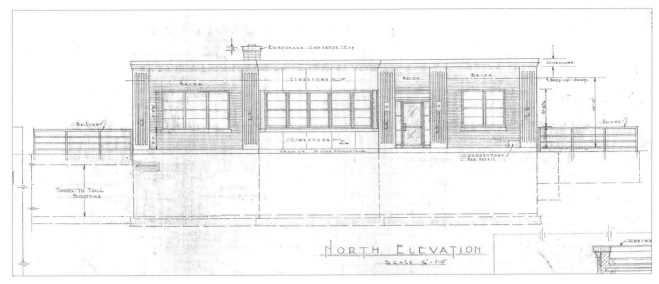

Fig. 19. Administration Building, Kingston-Rhinecliff Bridge. Halverson elevation, FHK.

in Haledon-Paterson, New Jersey, was also modern. Tobie Geertsma, in his "Dining Out" column, contrasted "old-fashioned" roadside diners with Park Diner's sleek "chrome and formica," tempered by "gold-spattered tile ... dark imitation woods ... [and] chandeliers [that] emulate elegance."[17]

Kingston Plaza Shopping Center, with a Grand Union supermarket, was developed by local businessman Robert H. Herzog and opened in 1964 below North

Front Street on land once occupied by the New York, Ontario & Western Railway. Britts department store (fig. 22) advertised itself as the largest store in the new shopping center, "comparable with 'big city' stores ... so modern, colorful, it's breathtaking. A glamorous gold, white and beige wonderland. Accented with original murals by a famous artist"—unfortunately unnamed. In 1966 Sears built a retail store and car service station, part of the great "building boom" of that year. Prior to Sears's

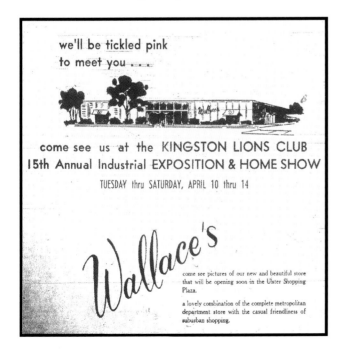

Left: Fig. 20. Wallace's, Ulster Shopping Center. Advertisement, KDF, Apr. 9, 1962. Fig. 21. Above: Park Diner (in 1983, Your Kettle Restaurant and Diner). Photograph, WBR.

Above: Fig. 22. Britts, Kingston Plaza Shopping Center. Advertisement, KDF, Apr. 15, 1964. Right: Fig. 23. Sears, Kingston Plaza Shopping Center. Advertisement, KDF, Nov. 2, 1966.

opening, an ad featured a Georgian Colonial–style doorframe with broken pediment (fig. 23) and announced, "Your New Sears in Kingston, America's First Colonial-Style Complete Sears Department Store."[18]

Kingston was then styling itself "a Colonial City," and civic leaders were urging that Kingston adopt a Colonial appearance to set itself apart from the uniform, mass culture of modern America. The Ulster County Historical Society, probably in the person of the editor of its journal, Harry Rigby, Jr., who was also Kingston City Historian, noted with pleasure that "tentative plans for the Sears Roebuck building in the Kingston Plaza were changed ... for Colonial architecture." Even more dramatically, "at the very last moment, the Savings and Loan Association of Kingston threw out plans for a functional building and instead built a beautiful structure of Colonial design." This return to the Colonial seemed to be motivated by "a search for individual identity on the part of Americans who almost despairingly have concluded that they are about to become nothing more than an eleven-digit telephone number, a postal zip code number, a Social Security and Internal Revenue identity number and an IBM number on their credit cards."

Could any of those despairing Americans have been IBMers involved with creating these numbers?

An important civic leader was Fred J. Johnston, a nationally prominent dealer in antiques. Since 1938

Fig. 24. Wall Street shop of Fred J. Johnston. c. 1970. Photograph, FHK.

Johnston had preserved the historic John Sudam house (c. 1812), a fine example of the Federal style, which functioned as his shop and home at the corner of Main and Wall Streets, opposite historic Old Dutch Church. In 1960 Johnston erected a new shop (fig. 24) on Wall Street next to the c. 1812 house and chose local architect Albert E. Milliken (1900–1978) to design the shop in a compatible Federal style. (Albert's architect son Robert recalls that his father and Johnston were "of similar minds" and had a long association, with Johnston storing antiques in a barn on Milliken's property during World War II.) Then, in 1966, when Sears was choosing a new Colonial exterior, Milliken provided, apparently "at the very last moment," a Georgian Colonial façade for the Savings and Loan Association of Kingston at 267 Wall Street (fig. 25), next door to Johnston's shop. Milliken, trained at Cornell in the 1920s, was adept at a variety of styles, but Robert Milliken proposes that his father's "basic interest was in the Colonial."[19]

For the 1960 reconstruction of the Kingston Savings Bank at 373 Wall Street, Milliken designed a façade combining stripped classical piers and cornice with broad areas of glass. But "Georgian Colonial" architecture was the choice for the Savings and Loan, a choice endorsed by its president, Alfred D. Ronder, Fred Johnston, and of course Milliken, who expressed the hope that Colonial would be widely adopted during the then-current Uptown Urban Renewal project. Johnston proclaimed the cause with particular passion: the Stockade area, including his establishment and 267 Wall Street, "has known the presence of some of the most illustrious names in American history. If all the exteriors of the buildings in this area were designed in the Colonial manner with the 20th century interior for convenience of modern living, then

Fig. 25. Savings & Loan Association of Kingston, 267 Wall Street. Photograph 2013 by Stephen Benson.

the uptown business section would become a unique and outstanding section of the city, the state, and the country."[20]

In 1969 Johnston advocated adoption of John Pike's plan to add Colonial porches to the late-nineteenth-century commercial buildings on Wall Street (fig. 26). Johnston proposed that the Colonial aspect might resemble the renowned restoration of Colonial Williamsburg, Virginia, but there would be more business activity in Kingston. Pike was aided by Albert Milliken. According to Robert Milliken, his father made drawings for the Pike Plan, which was a "pet project" of his father. (Milliken admired Pike, a noted Woodstock watercolorist, and Pike made a drawing for publication from Milliken's sketch of the "Georgian Colonial" Stone Ridge branch of the Kerhonkson National Bank.) Pike's scheme was carried out in the early 1970s, and in 1976 tourists were advised by *The New York Times* to shop "along Wall Street [where] the sidewalks are covered with a Colonial colonnaded overhang."[21]

Fig 26. Wall Street with Colonial porches added according to the Pike Plan. Photograph c. 1992–94 by Phyllis McCabe.

Johnston's advocacy of Colonial design was coupled with opposition to modern design. He told the Uptown Businessmen's Association, men who might be attracted to something up-to-date and modern: "Modern architecture dates itself. ... It could be out of style in a few years. Colonial architecture will last." The Uptown building whose modernity has asserted itself for fifty years and continues to antagonize Colonial enthusiasts is the Ulster County Office Building, designed by Augustus Schrowang, Jr. and Sr. The Schrowangs' six-story, steel-framed, metal-and-glass-curtain-wall, International-Style building (1962–64; fig. 27) vanquished brick Georgian designs put forward by Harry Halverson since the 1940s. Schrowang, Sr. was adept at designing Colonial houses, but his White Eagle Hall (opened 1961; a Polish-American social organization at 477 Delaware Ave.; fig. 28) displays the flat, simple geometric shapes characteristic of the International Style,

Fig. 27. Ulster County Office Building. Photograph 2013 by Stephen Benson.

only embellished with colored panels as found in schools of the 1950s. Schrowang, Jr. adapted the Ulster County Office Building design from a project he completed as an architecture student at Pratt Institute where his instructors were disciples of Bauhaus/International-Style masters Walter Gropius and Marcel Breuer. (Did Jr., who received his undergraduate degree from Pratt in 1959 and joined his father's firm in 1960, play a role in the design of the White Eagle Hall as well?) Negative criticism of the County Office Building was stirred up on local radio station WGHQ by Harry Thayer, who ridiculed it (and its occupants) as "The Glass Menagerie." The young architect,

Fig. 28. White Eagle Hall. Photograph 2013 by Stephen Benson.

however, influenced by his training at Pratt, had no interest in abandoning "honest" expression of materials and the times by reverting to "fake" Colonial.[22]

During the upheaval of Urban Renewal in Rondout during the 1960s, the Schrowang firm also designed the Rondout Neighborhood Center (1967–73; fig. 29) at 103 Broadway, where the Orpheum Theatre had once stood. Construction of the RNC for the city, including a recreation center and social service agencies, was supported by Senator Jacob Javits and funds from the Department of Housing and Urban Development. In contrast to the County Office Building, the walls here, of brick, seem formidable, almost fortress-like, although the rounding of the façade's corners softens the effect. Schrowang completed only the first story; the Neighborhood Center was completed by the Milliken firm, following the Schrowang design. (Plans for the completion, drawn by Robert E. Milliken and dated Jan. 16, 1973, are in the City Engineer's office.) Why the Schrowangs were replaced remains a mystery, although Robert Milliken recalls that local architects at the time were "competitive" and "not particularly friendly."[23]

Milliken was selected to design, across Broadway from the Neighborhood Center, a new City Hall (1968–71; fig. 30) on Garraghan Drive (named for Raymond W. Garraghan, the mayor who backed the city hall project, which was called by some, "Ray's Dream"). Milliken's building would replace the Victorian Gothic-style City Hall (1873–75) of Arthur Crooks on Broadway in Midtown. Adhering to the Colonial City theme he had followed in the Savings & Loan Association building on Wall Street, Milliken gave the low, one-story front a modest, white-columned Colonial portico. Ada Louise Huxtable, noted architectural critic for *The New York Times*, lambasted the new City Hall, calling it a "would-be Colonial structure ... that resembles a suburban supermarket or a turnpike-side Howard Johnson's more than a seat of government." Huxtable mistakenly understood that the old City Hall, endowed with "honest materials and sturdy style," had been demolished. Many thoughtful Kingstonians came to agree with Huxtable's preference for the Victorian City Hall, and between 1998 and 2000 it was restored and returned to use. Its impressive scale and prominent site made it appear a

Fig. 29. Rondout Neighborhood Center. Photograph 2013 by Stephen Benson.

Fig. 30. Former Kingston City Hall. Photograph 2013 by Stephen Benson.

more appropriate home of city government, and taste had come around to admire the vigorous color and detail of Victorian Gothic, while the Colonial Revival seemed timid and bland. (Milliken's City Hall now houses the City Court and Police Department.)[24]

Next door to Milliken's Colonial Revival City Hall is the modern Rondout Fire Station No. 3 (1969–71; fig. 31) by Harry Halverson's firm, Halverson-McCullough Associates. In 1940 Halverson had designed Colonial Revival quarters for Saugerties firemen in the Municipal Building, but thirty years later it seems that the economies of modernism and widespread acceptance of modern design resulted in acceptance of the sharp-planed, angular structure.[25]

As IBM brought tremendous growth to the Town of Ulster, Milliken made plans over several years for an

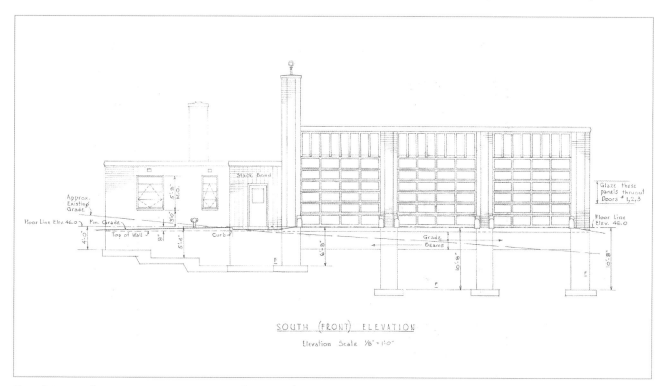

Fig. 31. Rondout Fire Station No. 3. Halverson elevation, FHK.

appropriate town hall. Would it reflect the modern image IBM had embraced tentatively in its Administration Building and then more completely in the Engineering Laboratory? Milliken himself had used the modern idiom (combined with traditional granite facing) in designing the Rondout Savings Bank (1967; fig. 32) at 300 Broadway. (The bank's previous, classical-style bank [1928] at 26 Broadway was demolished by Urban Renewal.) Or would it reveal the architect's preference for the Colonial Revival, a preference shared by many Americans at the time? Milliken's 1968 drawing (fig. 33) depicts a one-story town hall composed of three gable-roofed sections, one fitted with a white Colonial porch similar to the porch giving a measure of dignity to Kingston's City Hall. Voters turned down the project, probably objecting to the $300,000 expense of the office building and garage, not to the Colonial design. Today's Town of Ulster Office Building (1975; Anita G. Yuran, architect; fig. 34) is an example of low-budget modern—a "pre-engineered structure" manufactured by Stran-Steel—and not very expressive of a proud and prospering community.[26]

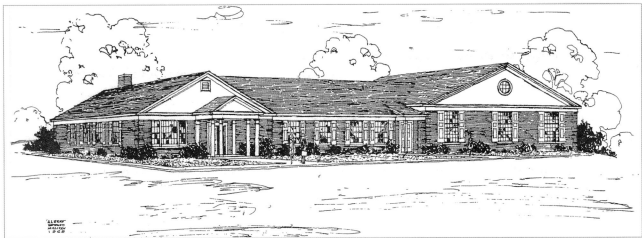

Fig. 33. Milliken proposal for Ulster Town Hall. Courtesy of Ulster Town Clerk.

Left: Fig. 34. Town of Ulster Office Building. Photograph 2013 by Stephen Benson. Below: Fig. 35. Hasbrouck Park School (John F. Kennedy Elementary School). Photograph of Halverson rendering, FHK.

On the other hand, new schools in the city and neighboring towns for Kingston City Schools (Consolidated) were both numerous and well-built, suggestive of civic pride—if not very adventuresome. Harry Halverson was responsible for several Kingston schools in the 1960s, but recalled, in retirement, that state regulations allowed little individuality. Using stock plans from the state architect, but still retaining Halverson as architect, was said to save $35,000 in building the Hasbrouck Park elementary school. A rendering of the Hasbrouck Park School (John F. Kennedy Elementary School, opened 1965; fig. 35) closely resembles one of the Merilina Avenue (Edson) Elementary School (1965–66; fig. 36), and both are credited to Harry Halverson & Associates. The formula, also seen in a modified version at Halverson's Zena Elementary School (1967–70)

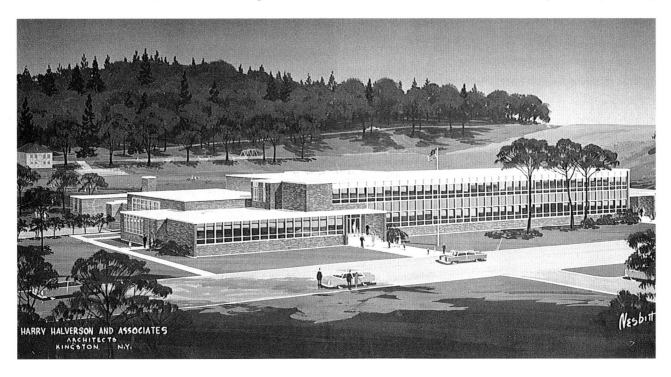

HARRY HALVERSON AND ASSOCIATES
ARCHITECTS
KINGSTON N.Y.

Fig. 36. Merilina Avenue School (Edson Elementary School). Photograph of Halverson rendering, FHK.

Fig. 37. M. Clifford Miller Junior High School. Photograph 2013 by Stephen Benson.

and the larger M. Clifford Miller Junior High School (1965–68; fig. 37), involved strictly modern and plain forms, not even the stripped classical or Georgian forms of his George Washington School.[27] Flat, rectangular brick walls were interrupted by grids of metal-framed windows, some with colored spandrels providing visual interest.

In 1956–57 Schrowang in association with Sherwood, Mills & Smith, a Connecticut firm experienced in school planning, designed (but did not complete) a large, thousand-pupil junior high school to stand on Joy's Lane, near Dietz Stadium. The design used the vocabulary of modern, International-Style forms common in schools of the period, simple geometric forms which Schrowang would use in his White

Eagle Hall and County Office Building. For the design of the Chambers School (1957), Milliken was obliged to use modern and associate with a larger firm, LaPierre, Litchfield of New York. On his own, Milliken designed the new St. Joseph's School (1962) with no external reference to traditional Christian architecture. In the early 1960s the highly regarded firm of Perkins & Will, located in Chicago and White Plains, was called upon to design additions to rural and city schools, as well as furnish plans for completely new schools in the city. Their "cheerful and modern" Sophie Finn School (1962; fig. 38) on Mary's Avenue exhibits a distinctive façade, thanks to the regular pattern of brick headers projecting from the brick wall cantilevered over the entrance. Perkins & Will replaced Schrowang as architect of the new school near Dietz Stadium (J. Watson Bailey Junior High). The site was moved from Joy's Lane to a wooded area adjacent to Forsyth Park. Just before opening in 1963, the school was described as a "graceful, two-winged, split-level building which incorporates ... some of the latest advances in school architecture." These included "completely modern laboratories for biology and earth science ... a completely equipped electronics language lab ... [and] a lovely auditorium." (Another Midwestern firm, Marshall Erdman & Associates, of Madison, Wisconsin, erected the Pine Street Professional Park [1965; fig. 39] whose horizontal lines and roof overhang stem from Frank Lloyd Wright. Erdman had built Wright's First Unitarian Society [1949–50] in Madison.)[28]

The Stone Ridge campus of Ulster County Community College, whose growth was aided by the presence of IBM, was designed in two phases. The first (1963–) is credited to the Schrowangs with consultant William N. Breger, who had been an assistant to the renowned German-American modern architect Walter Gropius and was currently Chairman of the Department of Architectural Design at Pratt Institute where the younger Schrowang had studied. Schrowang stressed that the new campus would be "a strong statement in the contemporary design idiom." The stark planes originally composing Macdonald DeWitt Library (fig. 40), the campus's centerpiece, certainly made a strong statement. However, the Schrowangs were replaced by the Milliken firm for the second phase (1967–), which included a computer center.

Fig. 38. Sophie Finn School. Photograph 2013 by Stephen Benson.

Fig. 39. Pine Street Professional Park. Photograph 2013 by Stephen Benson.

Thomas Clancy (1924–2012), an architect in Milliken's office, had a leading role in phase two. Robert Milliken recalls that the selection of architects (by the College Board of Trustees and County Supervisors) was based on "political" considerations and that Edgar Tafel, a Frank Lloyd Wright disciple, was interviewed for phase two but rejected as an out-of-towner.[29] Modern had been adopted by the Schrowangs, thus determining that modern would be used in the second phase. Colonial never seems to have been considered for Kingston's schools or the community college in the later '50s and '60s.

Kingston was well supplied with churches and synagogues when IBM arrived, but the decline of Rondout encouraged its synagogues to depart for Uptown, closer to their members' homes. Temple Emanuel moved to 243 Albany Avenue and a modern temple (1956–59; fig. 41) by architect Arthur I. Silver of New York City, with metalwork by Kurt Matzdorf, a renowned silversmith and professor at SUNY New Paltz. The street façade proclaims Jewish faith in the Hebrew text with English translation, "In Thy Light Do We See Light," and in sculptured emblems including representations of science and the arts, as well as prayer and Torah study. The sanctuary walls are a terra-cotta grill, designed by Silver, shielding a

membrane of colorful glass that admits colored light to the interior. Some years after departing their former, round-arched Romanesque/Moorish temple on Abeel Street, its large, circular, stained-glass window (fig. 42) with the Star of David was given a place of honor inside its successor. Arthur Silver's success at Temple Emanuel attracted the attention of Woodstock Methodists, who chose him to design Overlook Methodist Church (1963–68) on Route 212. While the church was of "contemporary" or modern design, its forty-two-foot belfry stemmed from Christian tradition and its bluestone facing connected it to the local heritage of bluestone quarrying.[30]

Congregation Ahavath Israel's modern synagogue (1965–66; fig. 43) at 100 Lucas Avenue was completed during the 1966 "building boom." It was planned by Harris Aaron Sanders, an Albany architect who had designed an IBM office building in Schenectady. The congregation had previously occupied a former Episcopal church on Wurts Street in Rondout, a building whose Gothic forms identified it with Christianity. The Sanders design had nothing overtly Gothic or Christian and is comparable to the modern design of Temple Beth Emeth (1957) in Albany, by Percival Goodman, the foremost architect of postwar American synagogues. The gable-roofed façade

plays solid masonry walls against a recessed angular wooden prow topped with glass. Hebrew letters standing for the Ten Commandments and a menorah sculpture clearly identify the function of the building.[31]

The city saw little new church construction during the IBM era. A small modern building was erected

Fig. 42. Window from Temple Emanuel's previous building on Abeel Street. Photograph 2013 by Stephen Benson.

during the 1966 building boom at 90 Millers Lane for the Christian and Missionary Alliance Church. In 1956 Harry Halverson planned a Georgian Colonial church for St. Mark's A.M.E. Church (fig. 44) on Foxhall Avenue, but it was never built.[32]

Fair Street Reformed turned to William Van Benschoten for its Christian Education Building (1956; fig. 45), whose boxy, modern shape was offset by rugged stone masonry on the Fair Street façade to accord with the limestone walls of the adjoining church (1850). Van Benschoten, an Episcopalian, served on the Commission on Church Building for the Episcopal Diocese of New York and designed modern churches in outlying towns: St. Gregory's Episcopal Church (1955–59), Woodstock, whose A-frame front was filled with translucent polyester panels (color design by artist Doris Lee) and a forty-five-foot wooden cross; and the Episcopal Church of Christ the King (1958–59) between High Falls and Stone Ridge. More remarkable is his St. George Greek Orthodox Church (1962–64; fig. 46) at 294 Greenkill Avenue, which combined Byzantine architectural influence—the sequence of narthex (interior porch), nave, and domed sanctuary—with contemporary needs (for example, a basement auditorium and kitchen, site of popular Greek

Fig. 43. Synagogue of Congregation Ahavath Israel, 100 Lucas Avenue. Photograph 2013 by Stephen Benson.

Festival dining). The façade bears a striking mosaic (fig. 47) of St. George and the Dragon "In Memory of Stephen P. Larios," a founder of the Kingston church who was given the honor of naming it St. George.[33]

Despite his essential commitment to modernism, Van Benschoten was a member of the Holland Society and the Ulster County Historical Society, and a key advisor to the Junior League survey of historic Ulster County architecture, which resulted in the useful book, *Early Architecture of Ulster County* (1974). After his death in an auto accident in 1968, Van Benschoten was cited as "the one person who was a prime mover in the survey and who recognized the needs for its completion."[34]

George V. Hutton (1928–2008; fig. 48), a Kingston native and, like Van Benschoten, a modern architect trained at Yale, also played a key role in historic preservation locally. As a young modernist who had worked in the offices of Eero Saarinen and Paul Rudolph, Hutton planned a renovation and addition (1967–68; fig. 49) to the Kingston Savings Bank, which had been reconstructed by Milliken in 1960.

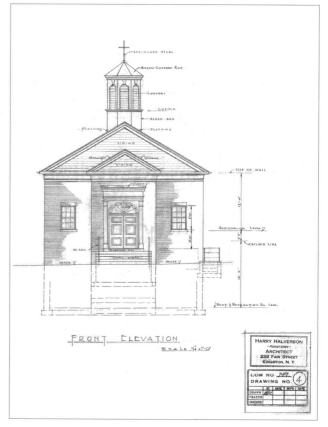

Fig. 44. St. Mark's A.M.E. Church. Halverson proposed elevation, FHK.

Above: Fig. 45. Christian Education Building, Fair Street Reformed Church. At bottom: Fig. 46. St. George Greek Orthodox Church. At right: Fig. 47. St. George and the Dragon, mosaic. Photographs 2013 by Stephen Benson.

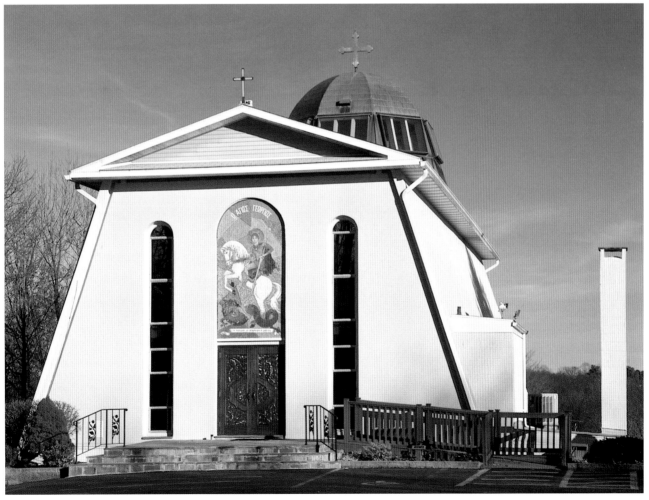

Most intriguing is the narrow, walled passage between Wall Street and the parking lot at the rear of the building, which furnishes pedestrians a distant glimpse of the historic DAR house or, for those walking in the opposite direction, a bit of Old Dutch Church. Was Hutton inspired by walking explorations of old European towns, or by passageways on the Yale campus? Here and in his Wiltwyck Fire Station (1977; fig. 50), next to the ruinous stone house on Frog Alley, Hutton employed stark, geometric forms with no revival of historic ornament. Yet he made a distinct contribution to the cause of architectural preservation in Kingston as one of the initial members (along with Fred Johnston) of the city's Landmarks Preservation Commission and service on the board of the Friends of Historic Kingston. In addition, Governor Nelson Rockefeller appointed Hutton to the board championing the preservation of Frederic Church's Olana.[35] Finally, toward the end of his life, he researched and wrote a valuable history, *The Great Hudson River Brick Industry* (2003), in which earlier generations of Huttons played an important role.

In the mid-1970s, during the women's movement, women were at last receiving recognition as creative architects. Frances Halsband, trained at Columbia and since 1972 a founding partner in the distinguished firm of Kliment Halsband Architects, was chosen to design a substantial addition (1975–78; fig. 51) to the Shingle-Style house occupied by the YWCA at 209 Clinton Avenue. She recalls that the YWCA interviewed George Hutton for the commission, but probably preferred a woman architect, and that architecturally enlightened IBMers in Woodstock supported her in gaining the commission. However, an influential woman living nearby opposed a vigorously modern

Fig. 50. Wiltwyck Fire Station. Photograph 2013 by Stephen Benson.

Fig. 51. Frances Halsband's addition to the YWCA. Photograph by Norman McGrath. Courtesy of Kliment Halsband Architects.

design. Given this constraint, Halsband made the interior of the addition more "adventurous" than the exterior.[36]

In the end, it seems that IBM's use of modern design had little impact on buildings erected in the area for clients other than IBM. Neither modern nor Colonial won a decisive victory in Kingston and vicinity during the IBM years. Robert Milliken believes that his father would have preferred to focus on designing Colonial houses, but that to keep the office running he needed to take on school, commercial, and institutional commissions where modern was required in the 1960s and '70s; Milliken designed the "ultra-modern 36-unit" Motel 19 (1964) near the Thruway's exit 19, as well as the Ulster County Infirmary (1968–) and Jail at Golden Hill (1969–). So it would have been a pleasure for Milliken to plan the Wiltwyck Golf Clubhouse (1955–56; fig. 52) with its two-story, Colonial porch. Even more satisfying must have been the Hurley branch of the Kerhonkson National Bank (1963; fig. 53) where Milliken altered an existing wooden house to resemble an eighteenth-century Hurley stone house. He

Fig. 52. Wiltwyck Golf Clubhouse. Milliken rendering. Courtesy of Wiltwyck Golf Club.

incorporated stones from an old, ruinous Schoonmaker house in Accord, while employing as mason Stanley Hasbrouck, Jr. (1927–2014) from one of New Paltz's founding families.[37] The bank's customers surely included IBMers who would have looked askance at a glass-and-steel bank building in the midst of quaint old Hurley. ⊙

William B. Rhoads, a professor emeritus of Art History at SUNY New Paltz, is the author of Kingston, New York: The Architectural History & Guide *(Black Dome Press and Friends of Historic Kingston, 2003) and* Ulster County, New York: The Architectural History & Guide *(Black Dome Press, 2011). Since 1969 much of his scholarship has focused on the Colonial Revival in American architecture.*

Fig. 53. Hurley Branch, Kerhonkson National Bank. Milliken elevation. Courtesy of Robert E. Milliken.

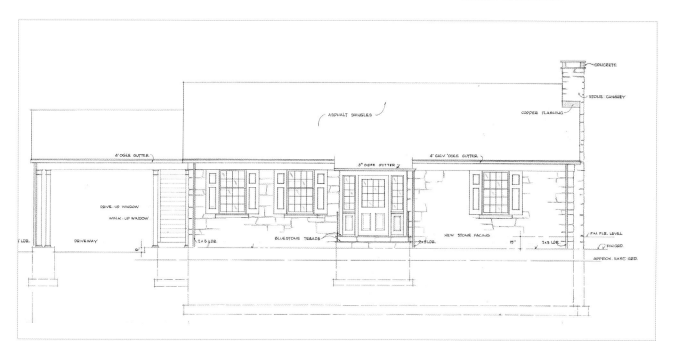

Notes

1. William B. Rhoads, "The Long and Unsuccessful Effort to Kill Off the Colonial Revival," in *Re-creating the American Past* (Charlottesville: University of Virginia Press, 2006), 17; William B. Rhoads, *Teller & Halverson* (Friends of Historic Kingston, 2005), 31.

2. *Kingston Daily Freeman* (hereafter *KDF*), June 5, 1952, June 22, 1953, Sept. 23, 1955, July 2, 1957. These and subsequent references to articles in the *Freeman* were obtained by searching the extremely useful fultonhistory.com.

3. Dawn Stanford of the IBM Corporate Archives identified Charles Higgins as architect of the Endicott building; Harvey Flad e-mail to author, Feb. 26, 2014; George S. Koyl, ed., *American Architects Directory* (New York: Bowker, 1962), 600; *Architectural Record*, v. 45, Feb. 1949, 96–103.

4. Harvey K. Flad and Clyde Griffen, *Main Street to Mainframes: Landscape and Social Change in Poughkeepsie* (Albany: Excelsior, 2009), 174–175; "Dedication of a Plant at Kingston," *Business Machines, General Section*, Nov. 20, 1956, 2–4, and "Welcome," IBM brochure, perhaps for the Nov. 2, 1956, dedication, both read at the Friends of Historic Kingston (hereafter, FHK).

5. *KDF*, Aug. 11, 1958; IBM press release, "Kingston IBM Laboratory to Add 250,000 Square-Foot Facility," FHK; *50 Years of Collecting: Art at IBM* (New York: IBM Gallery of Science and Art, 1989), unpaged; Paul Goldberger, "Corporate Design That Stays on the Safe Side," *The New York Times*, May 13, 1990.

6. *KDF*, Dec. 31, 1966.

7. *Kingston City Directory*, various years; Robert Milliken in conversation with author, Nov. 21, 2013.

8. Anthony Robinson, *Home Again Home Again* (New York: William Morrow, 1969), 17–18, 38–39, 183–192.

9. Gail Godwin, *The Finishing School* (New York: Viking, 1984), 20–21, 109, 151.

10. Kingston City Directories, various years; e-mails to author from Lowell Thing, Oct. 30 and Dec. 10, 2013, and from Jane Kellar, Oct. 30 and Dec. 11, 2013; author's conversation with the Oseas, Dec. 13, 2013. Jerry Leatherman, an IBMer, and Ruth Scogna, wife of Paul Scogna, another IBMer, both served as treasurer of the Friends of Historic Kingston and maintained older houses as their residences—Leatherman a 1920s Tudor Revival house at 261 Pearl St., and Scogna the historic stone Dumond House at 147 Green St. John T. Murphy, who had a 35-year career with IBM, and his wife Patricia O'Reilly Murphy maintained their home at 19 Irving Place. Pat, who grew up at 55 West Chestnut Street, has long been a leader in the Friends of Historic Kingston. Pat's cousin, John Falvey, an IBMer, lived with his wife Ila (active in FHK) on West Chestnut Street, and John informed fellow IBMer Lowell Thing that 55 West Chestnut was for sale. Pat Murphy e-mail to author, Dec. 16, 2013. Raymond J. Armater, who retired after 36 years with IBM, was a long-time president of the Ulster County Historical Society. *Times-Herald-Record*, Jan. 23, 1991; Godwin, *Finishing School*, 165.

11. *The New York Times*, Aug. 26, 1956; *KDF*, Nov. 15, 1956, Mar. 15 and May 31, 1957, May 12, 1959; "Levitt Adds 1950 Model to His Line," *Life*, v. 28, May 22, 1950, 141; Barbara M. Kelly, *Expanding the American Dream: Building and Rebuilding Levittown* (Albany: State University of New York Press, 1993), 80–82. For Poughkeepsie IBMer housing, see Larson Fisher Associates, "Reconnaissance-level Historic Resource Survey Update for Town of Poughkeepsie Historical Commission," September 2011.

12. Author's phone conversations with Gaynel Tavares, Jan. 2 and 25, 2014; *The New York Times*, May 5 and July 21, 1957, Feb. 28, 1960; Saugerties High School, *The Sawyer*, 1965.

13. *KDF*, Feb. 5, 1964; Godwin, *The Finishing School*, 178.

14. E-mails from John DeJoy to Ward Mintz, Dec. 11 and 12, 2013; John DeJoy in conversation with author at DeJoy's house, Dec. 12, 2013; website of "Edmond G. Loedy, Architect P.C."; for Copley's Accord house, see Jean Strouse, "In Tune with the Forest," *Architectural Digest*, Oct. 2007.

15. Halverson's plans for Snyder house, Commission 765, at FHK; *The New York Times*, Mar. 11, 2011; for "The Jetsons," see Wikipedia; Kayla Feldman e-mail to Ward Mintz, Dec. 10, 2013; *KDF*, Nov. 11, 1964 and Mar. 7, 1966. The open space below the Abelove house functions as a carport, as did the space below a similar modern house pictured on the cover of the popular *Second Treasury of Contemporary Houses* (New York: Dodge, 1959). Breuer's house was moved to the Rockefeller estate at Pocantico Hills where, beginning in 1950, it served as a guest house; it has been restored in recent years. Diana Budds, "Restoring Breuer's House in Garden," www.dwell.com.

16. *KDF*, May 10, 1957 and July 10, 1959; Halverson's plans for bridge buildings, Commission 742, at FHK.

17. *KDF*, Dec. 30, 1961, Jan. 4 and Apr. 9, 1962, May 15, 1963 and Nov. 8, 1969. George Kakoulis and George Zidro owned the diner. In 1968 Zidro was treasurer of the local chapter of the Order of AHEPA,

which met in St. George Greek Orthodox Church, described below. *KDF*, Feb. 15, 1968.

18. *KDF*, Dec. 31, 1963, April 13 and 15, 1964, Aug. 13, 1965, Mar. 17 and Nov. 2, 1966. Augustus Schrowang, Jr., mentioned to the author, Aug. 1, 2007, that the shopping center design began as one of his student projects at Pratt Institute.

19. Sophie Miller in *KDF*, Mar. 1, 1963; *KDF*, June 23, 1966; "At Long Last!", *Ulster County Gazette*, v. 4, July 1966, 2, 8; author's conversation with Robert Milliken, Nov. 21, 2013 (hereafter, Milliken 2013).

20. *KDF*, Sept. 23, 1965. In 1966 Johnston also gave his seal of approval to Harry Halverson's conversion of an ordinary storefront at 632 Broadway into something Colonial for First Federal Savings & Loan. *KDF*, Dec. 12, 1966. The conversion is no longer evident.

21. *KDF*, Dec. 4, 1969; Milliken 2013; *KDF*, May 17, 1957; Harold Faber, "The Apple Picking Season Opens," *The New York Times*, Sept. 17, 1976. The colonnades were recently restored, not without controversy.

22. *KDF*, Dec. 4, 1969, Dec. 21, 1962, July 25, 1964, June 13, 1961; Augustus Schrowang, Jr., in conversation with author, Aug. 1, 2007, and his e-mail to author, May 15, 2009, and letter to author, Feb. 7, 2012. *The Glass Menagerie* (1944) was Tennessee Williams's first successful play. Robert Milliken believes that while Halverson's Georgian design would have been "more fitting," the county "got a lot of building for their money, and the building has served well." Milliken 2013.

23. Schrowang e-mail to author, Aug. 4, 2007; *KDF*, Oct. 24, 1967, and Feb. 10, 1968; Milliken 2013.

24. *KDF*, Jan. 8 and Feb. 25, 1969; Edwin Millard Ford, *Street Whys* (Round Top: Ford Printing, 2010), 116; Huxtable, "The Public Building: From Soaring Statements to Shoddy Mediocrity," *The New York Times*, Nov. 10, 1974.

25. *KDF*, Dec. 15, 1969; Halverson's plans for Rondout Fire Station, Commission 845, at FHK; William B. Rhoads, *Ulster County, New York: The Architectural History & Guide* (Delmar: Black Dome Press, 2011), 205.

26. *KDF*, Dec. 6, 1956, Nov. 14, 1967; "Proposal to the Residents of the Town of Ulster for Town Office Building and Town Garage," brochure in Town Clerk's office; *KDF*, Oct. 2, 1968; blueprints, Nov. 30, 1975, in Town Clerk's office.

27. Author's conversation with Harry Halverson, Nov. 14, 1984; *KDF*, May 3, 1962, Apr. 26, 1963, June 18, 1965; photos commissioned by Halverson of his schools at FHK; correspondence between Halverson's firm and Kingston City Schools regarding Zena School, 1967–70, and M. Clifford Miller Junior High School, 1965–68, remains at KCS and was made available to the author by Anna Brett and Ward Mintz.

28. *KDF*, June 26, 1956, and Apr. 18, 1957; 1957 brochure regarding the junior high e-mailed by Schrowang, May 1, 2013; *KDF*, June 6, 1957, Feb. 26, 1962, May 4 and Aug. 20, 1963, Sept. 2, 1965; William Allin Storrer, *The Frank Lloyd Wright Companion* (Chicago: University of Chicago Press, 1993), 301.

29. *KDF*, Sept. 13, 1963, Aug. 27, 1964, Apr. 15, 1965, Nov. 18, 1966, and June 13, 1967; Milliken 2013. The first phase included a "Business Machines Laboratory." See c. 1965 brochure, "The New Campus for Ulster County Community College," at its DeWitt Library.

30. *KDF*, May 1 and 18, 1959; Renee Silver e-mails to Ward Mintz, July 30 and 31, 2013; Jessica Fillmore e-mail to author, Jan. 14, 2014; *KDF*, Sept. 17, 1963, and Mar. 16, 1968.

31. *KDF*, Dec. 11, 1965; Koyl, *American Architects Directory*, 611; Diana S. Waite, ed., *Albany Architecture* (Albany: Mount Ida Press, 1993), 153; e-mail from Ward Mintz to author, Feb. 5, 2014.

32. *KDF*, Dec. 31, 1966, and June 20, 1967; Halverson's plans for Commission 747 at FHK.

33. *KDF*, Nov. 30, 1956, May 12, 1955, June 17, 1959, July 2, 1958, Mar. 12, 1959, Feb. 17, 1962, Dec. 23, 1964, Apr. 21, 1966 and Dec. 23, 1964. Van Benschoten's plans, kept at the church, are dated March to June 1964. An IBM administrative assistant, Jennie C. Chafouleas, was a founding member and parishioner of St. George. *KDF*, Feb. 12, 2014.

34. *KDF*, June 7, 1958, and Apr. 6, 1968.

35. *KDF*, Oct. 7, 1964, Aug. 22 and Sept. 26, 1968, Aug. 1, 1966, May 5, 1969. Plans for the fire station, dated 7-6-77, are in the collection of Sandra Hutton.

36. Frances Halsband, FAIA, in conversation, Mar. 22, 2013; www.kliment-halsband.com.

37. Milliken 2013; *KDF*, Sept. 14, 1964, July 12, 1968, and Aug. 15, 1969, July 20, 1955, Feb. 24, 1964.

ACKNOWLEDGMENTS: I would like to thank for their help in the research for and publication of this essay: Alan Adin, City Engineering Office; Frank Almquist; Susan Basch; Steve Benson; Anna Brett; the Rev. David L. Bronson; Judy Capurso, DeWitt Library, SUNY Ulster; Jason Cosenza, Ulster Town Clerk; John and Alice Cross; John DeJoy; Jessica Fillmore; Father Iakoeos Fitzpatrick, St. George Greek Orthodox Church; Harvey Flad; Edwin M. Ford; Steve Hoare; Sandra Hutton; Carol A. Johnson, Haviland-Heidgerd Historical Collection, Elting Memorial Library; Jane Kellar; *Kingston Daily Freeman*; Robert Milliken; Ward Mintz; Patricia O'Reilly Murphy; Jonathan and Iris Oseas; Sally Rhoads; Peter Roberts; Peter J. Savago; Augustus R. Schrowang; Renee Silver; Dawn Stanford, IBM Corporate Archives, Somers; Gaynel Tavares; and Lowell Thing.

A Timeline

By George G. Washington

Introduction

The building, construction and occupation of the massive new IBM location in the Kingston area was a major event for the city of Kingston and the surrounding area. In 1952 the upper Mid-Hudson Valley was a relatively quiet area, rural in nature, supported by apparel companies, a dying brick-making industry, agriculture, and other small businesses.

In 1995, when IBM Kingston was dissolved and the buildings sold, Kingston and nearby towns and villages had changed into a vibrant community with many new homes and small businesses and several massive shopping malls that made the Kingston area competitive with Poughkeepsie and Albany.

Over the forty-three years that the IBM Kingston plant and engineering laboratory were operational, significant events and discoveries were made by its employees that affected not only the Kingston area but the world at large. The design, development and manufacturing of the SAGE air defense system brought new technology and jobs to the Mid-Hudson Valley and provided the United States with computer systems installed in border states that could identify any hostile air attacks. The same set of people several years later delivered to American Airlines the SABRE reservation system, and several years after that the FAA nationwide aircraft control system.

IBM Kingston engineered, developed and manufactured the first interactive displays and software systems that over time would allow individuals to use computers the way we do today with our laptops and tablets. The application of interactive systems in merchandising retail stores was made possible by the efforts of the IBM Kingston engineering and manufacturing staff. IBM Kingston was a leader in the interconnection of computer systems and developed the products people needed to get their jobs done more easily and accurately.

The IBM Kingston plant and engineering laboratory were responsible for the creation of jobs and new opportunities for Kingston and Ulster County. The employees at the IBM Kingston location were inventive, empathetic to customer needs and highly intelligent. Their inventiveness produced many patented products. The Kingston area benefited from having these people in the community. The quality of school systems in the area improved, housing demand increased exponentially, and the IBM employees increased local demand for food, clothing, entertainment, and better restaurants.

The Kingston area was greatly enhanced by the presence of the IBM plant, and the IBM plant was greatly enhanced by the quality and dedication of the people that it hired from the local community. It was a win-win situation for both Kingston and IBM, and it is sad that that union has now been broken.

IBM and the Kingston Area 1952–1995

1952 IBM begins working with MIT's Lincoln Laboratories on Air Force defense computer.

1953 IBM is awarded contract to build the prototype computers XD1 and XD2.

1954 IBM is awarded primary computer hardware contract for the SAGE air defense system.
IBM begins construction on the Kingston site.

1955 IBM moves typewriter assembly to the Kingston plant, increasing the plant population
by an additional 1,900 employees.
XD2 prototype is installed in Kingston.
Assembly and testing begins on first AN/FSQ-7 Combat Direction Central.
IBM Kingston begins training of SAGE System Engineers.

1956 IBM Kingston ships the first SAGE system to be installed at McGuire AFB
in New Jersey.

1958 The Maguire AFB SAGE system becomes operational, communicating with the
Syracuse control system at Hancock Field.
IBM Kingston Custom Systems organization provides support to the Mercury Manned
Space Flight Program.

1959 IBM Kingston ships the last of the SAGE systems to Makah Air Force Base in
northwestern Washington State.
IBM Kingston site begins to train Air Force personnel to test and maintain installed
SAGE systems. The project is called Head Start.
The number of employees at IBM Kingston has increased beyond 5,000.
IBM field engineering has completed the training of over 1,850 field engineers
since 1955.
IBM Kingston assembles a transistorized version of the AN/FSQ-7for Colorado Springs.
IBM announces the 7090 computer system (a solid-state version of the AN/FSQ-7)
for commercial use.

1960 IBM Kingston begins the construction of the engineering laboratory across the street from the main building.

Montgomery Ward's begins construction on a new store on Route 9W behind the IBM Kingston facility.

1961 IBM Kingston delivers two IBM STRETCH computers to the U.S. Atomic Energy Commission.

IBM Kingston transfers the typewriter assembly process to the IBM plant in Kentucky.

IBM Kingston accepts the manufacturing responsibility for all IBM power supplies random access drums and core plane memory.

IBM Kingston Custom Systems organization provides major support to the Apollo Space Flight Control System to put men on the moon.

1962 IBM Kingston was designated the location for the computer center serving the entire IBM internal teleprocessing system.

IBM Kingston begins design and engineering of video display terminals for commercial delivery.

At the New York World's Fair, IBM demonstrates the language translating system developed and manufactured at Kingston.

The IBM Kingston–designed SABRE Airline Reservation system is installed by American Airlines.

1964 IBM Kingston announces the 2260 display terminal for attachment to the IBM System 360 processor line. Manufacturing of the display terminals will be done at the IBM Kingston plant.

1965 IBM Kingston begins final testing of System 360 computer systems prior to shipment to customers.

The Mayfair Theatre begins operation in the shopping center occupied by Montgomery Ward's behind IBM Kingston. The Mavis tire store is built adjacent to the theater.

1968 IBM Kingston begins design and engineering of the 3270 terminal system to replace the existing 2260 system.

1969 IBM Kingston manufacturing ships the first System 360 model 75 to Columbia University for Scientific Space Studies.

1970 IBM Kingston phases out the manufacturing of display terminals and control units that will henceforth be manufactured at the IBM Raleigh plant.

1971 IBM Kingston takes over responsibility for design and support for the IBM TSS (Time Sharing System) that will be announced as the IBM System 360 Model 67.

IBM Kingston starts construction of a 150,000-square-foot building to be called Building 005.

IBM Kingston announces the shipment of the 3270 display terminals.

1972 IBM Kingston announces and ships industry communications systems for market segments such as finance, banking and retail stores.

1973 IBM Kingston announces plans to build a 250,000-square-foot four-story engineering laboratory.

1975 3790 Distributed Systems Announcement with DPCX operating system. DPCX was IBM's distributed operating system to support a word processing application.

1976 thru 1981 IBM Kingston announces and delivers the 8100 Distributed System along with two separate operating systems DPPX for data applications and DPCX for word processing.

1985 IBM Kingston establishes a supercomputer support system for application development and marketing.

1987 IBM Kingston's gas panel project with Owens/Illinois and Illinois University is sold to Plasmarco of Highland, New York, and twenty years later is sold to Panasonic for their large-screen HD television products.

1990s The decade of the 1990s brings construction of many commercial buildings along Rte. 9W behind IBM Kingston. These include Red Lobster, Office Depot, Lowe's, Home Depot, and ShopRite, helping to make the Kingston area a commercial competitor to Albany and Poughkeepsie.

1990 IBM Kingston's community programs receive over $1,195,000 in contributions and matching grants.

1991 Construction completed of a pedestrian link over Neighborhood Road between IBM Kingston buildings 202 and the laboratory.

1995 IBM Kingston employees are transferred to Poughkeepsie or other locations or retired from the business.

George G. (Jerry) Washington worked for IBM for 35 years, starting as a Systems Field Engineer in 1956 for the SAGE system and ending his career in 1990 as a National Marketing Manager for Super Computers Applications for System 3090. His responsibilities in between varied from Product Planner to Assistant to the Site Director of Engineering. His career started and ended at the Kingston site, but he also worked in Denver, Colorado, Fort Lee, Virginia, and Houston, Texas.

THE CHAMP
Jewett captures
women's golf title
. . . page 17

**Onteora voters reject
budget propositions**
. . . page 3

Chance of a storm
Today's weather forecast calls for rain
and a chance of a thunderstorm. High
70 to 75. Details on page 3.

Daily Freeman

New York State Society of Newspaper Editors
1993
Newspaper
of the
YEAR

Kingston, N.Y.   Thursday, July 28, 1994   50¢

GOODBYE, IBM

A moving van drives past the IBM-Kingston facility on Wednesday hours after the plant's shutdown was announced.

Freeman photo by Bill Madden

Local site will close next year; no layoffs

By SANDRA FRINTON
Freeman staff

KINGSTON — IBM on Wednesday confirmed it will close its Kingston plant by the end of 1995 and transfer the remaining 1,500 employees to its Poughkeepsie site.

No layoffs will accompany the shutdown. Instead, the entire Ulster County workforce will move 26 miles south to the Dutchess County facility over the next 18 months.

The 39-year-old local plant, in the town of Ulster, has been the county's largest job producer and the backbone of the local economy for decades.

The closure was widely anticipated in a community that has seen the workforce at the 2.4 million-square-foot plant drop to its lowest level during the last two years.

At its peak, in 1985 and '86, IBM-Kingston employed 7,100 people. The combined population of the Kingston and Poughkeepsie plants now stands at 6,500. Both plants are involved in the production of mainframe computers.

The bulk of transfers to Poughkeepsie will take place in the first quarter of 1995, with some activity before that, said Frank Jones, IBM's Mid-Hudson Valley site general manager.

Top IBM officials said during a news conference Wednesday at the Kingston Holiday Inn that the decision, made Monday after months of analysis, came down to pure economics and available space.

"The logic behind our decision is compelling," said Nicholas M. Donofrio, IBM vice president and general manager of the Large Scale Computing Division. "Logic says we can't continue to operate two sites and be as competitive as we must be. But our history and hearts

(See **IBM**, page 16)

More IBM news...

On page 8:
- IBM's decision to vacate the Kingston plant may actually help in the effort to market the plant's 2.4 million square feet of available space.
- Local real estate officials don't expect Kingston IBM'ers to move to Poughkeepsie en masse when they are transferred.
- Like many area residents, U.S. Rep. Maurice Hinchey says IBM's decision to leave Ulster County comes as no surprise. And he's trying to secure funding to open this fall in the former Ulster Shopping Plaza.
- Lt. Gov. Stan Lundine and local leaders will hold a 4 p.m. news conference today at Kingston City Hall to discuss IBM and the Kingston-Ulster designation as an Economic Development Zone.
- Photos reflect the local atmosphere on "The strangest of days."

On page 9:
- Ulster County business leaders are ready to deal with life after IBM. Company officials, meanwhile, are optimistic about other tenants coming in and about their efforts to turn the Kingston site into a "viable business park."
- Employees of IBM-Kingston — once the backbone of the Ulster County economy — seem despondent about the future, and ex-employees say the shutdown was to be expected. "We knew it was going to happen. It was just a matter of time," says a computer operator who left the company last year.
- Business leaders in Northern Dutchess and Columbia County expect minimal impact from the Kingston plant's shutdown.
- IBM will continue to pay property taxes on its local plant, even after the last employee leaves.
- Plant chronology.

On page 14:
- Editorial

Meeting with reporters Wednesday are, from left, Ulster County Legislature Chairman Daniel Alfonso, Sen. William Larkin, Ulster Supervisor Frank Sottile and UCDC chief Richard Mathews.

Freeman photo by Bob Haines

Leaders hail economic zone

Designation offers development incentives for IBM-Kingston site

By KEVIN BARRY
and MICHAEL HAYES
Freeman staff

KINGSTON — Local officials hailed Gov. Mario Cuomo's announcement Wednesday that the town of Ulster and city of Kingston had won state designation as an Economic Development Zone. The announcement was made at the exact time officials were confirming plans to close the IBM-Kingston plant by 1995.

The governor, at a news conference in New York City, also announced approval of Dutchess County's application for an economic development zone. The zone will include parts of the city of Poughkeepsie and towns of Poughkeepsie and East Fishkill.

In all, 21 new zones will offer tax credits and other incentives for new or expanding businesses, bringing the total to 40 created since 1986.

Newburgh/Beacon and Ellenville/Wawarsing were among nine applicants statewide that did not receive the latest Economic Development Zone designation.

Kingston Mayor T.R. Gallo speaks at news conference with Assemblyman Kevin Cahill, D-Kingston, left, and Ulster Supervisor Frank Sottile.

Freeman photo by Bob Haines

> **'We will do everything possible to bring business into Kingston and Ulster and this Economic Development Zone will help out'**
> — *T.R. Gallo, Kingston mayor*

Cuomo said the program has helped create 4,500 jobs since 1987. He said he would ask the state Legislature to expand the program next year.

At a news conference at Kingston City Hall, Mayor T.R. Gallo called

(See **Economic**, page 16)

'This is not doomsday,' local officials declare

By ROBERT MITCHELL
Freeman staff

KINGSTON — The area's elected officials tried to put the best possible face on the announcement Wednesday that IBM will close its Kingston plant by the end of 1995.

"This is not gloom and doom as some of you would like to believe," Richard Mathews, chief executive officer of the Ulster County Development Corp., said during an afternoon news conference at the Holiday Inn.

Mathews, former chairman of the Ulster County Legislature, was

joined by several of the area's elected officials, who met Wednesday morning with Big Blue officials to discuss the situation.

Just moments before, IBM officials conducted a news conference in the same room and announced the long-rumored closure of the Kingston plant and the transfer of the remaining 1,500 employees to Poughkeepsie.

The officials said IBM's move will be softened by a state announcement that Kingston and the town of Ulster were granted state Economic

(See **Officials**, page 9)

Shutdown comes as another blow to stores, eateries

Some fear the worst; others expect to weather the storm

By SANDRA FRINTON
Freeman staff

TOWN OF ULSTER — To TCBY owner John Bassett, IBM-Kingston has been dead since the company laid off the bulk of its workforce a year-and-a-half ago.

The planned closing of the plant, which is walking distance from his yogurt shop on Morton Boulevard, can't have much more of a negative impact, he reasons. He's already felt the worst.

"I think we've hit bottom," he said. "It's like they've been non-existent over the past two years."

In better times, TCBY and other shops around the site thrived with the company. Nowadays, they pray for another company to come in with employees needing everything from lunch to a haircut.

"We need to light a candle and

say a prayer," Bassett said.

But Bassett remains optimistic. This summer, TCBY has begun to see sales rise again after being down 30 percent.

Daybreak Season Pizza, at 207 Boices Lane, across from the IBM plant, is hanging on despite a 40 percent drop in its lunch business. But owner Nike Psichas doesn't

know for how much longer.

"It makes us very nervous," she said. "We hoped someone else would come in by now. The longer they wait, it isn't good for us. We have to find a way to survive."

The remaining 1,500 employees at IBM-Kingston will help keep the business afloat in the near term. But an empty plant could spell

disaster for the 14-month-old pizzeria.

"We're optimistic that with so many buildings, someone will come in," said Psichas, who runs the pizzeria with husband, Dimitris. "It's just a matter of what happens until then."

Other service-orientated businesses that rely less on nearby walk-in traffic expected less of a negative impact.

(See **Businesses**, page 16)

IBM Kingston born as typewriter plant

IBM opened its Kingston plant with 1,000 employees in 1955 as a typewriter manufacturing facility. By 1962 production had shifted to computers, and the plant's population was on the rise.

Plant begins manufacturing 7040/7044 computer systems

Peak employment was 7,100 in 1985 and 1986

Plant will close by 1996

Source: IBM Kingston

Friday in Preview: Brubeck opens Bardavon's jazz series

Index

Workers assembling System 360 Power Subsystem units, early 1970s. Courtesy of IBM.

Manufacturing the 7044 Data Processing System, IBM Kingston, 1960s. Courtesy of IBM.